TOWN-PLANNING IN PATIALA STATE AND CITY:

A REPORT TO H.H. THE MAHARAJA OF PATIALA

PATRICK GEDDES

GYAN

Published by

Gyan Publishing House
5, Ansari Road
Daryaganj, New Delhi-110002
Phone: 011-47034999, 9811692060
E-mail: books@gyanbooks.com

Distribution Network
gyanbooks.com
India, USA, Canada, UK, Australia

ISBN: 978-93-7316-209-6 (PB)

First Published, 1922

2nd Impression 2025

Printed at: Gyan Press, Delhi.

TOWN-PLANNING IN PATIALA STATE AND CITY
Arthur: PATRICK GEDDES

TOWN-PLANNING IN PATIALA STATE AND CITY

Two Views in Desraj Street: (I) Present and (II) Possible.

(II) Proposed Improvement—Shed removed.

(I) Present State—Derelict Shed blocking traffic and hiding Mandir.

SKETCH PLANS.

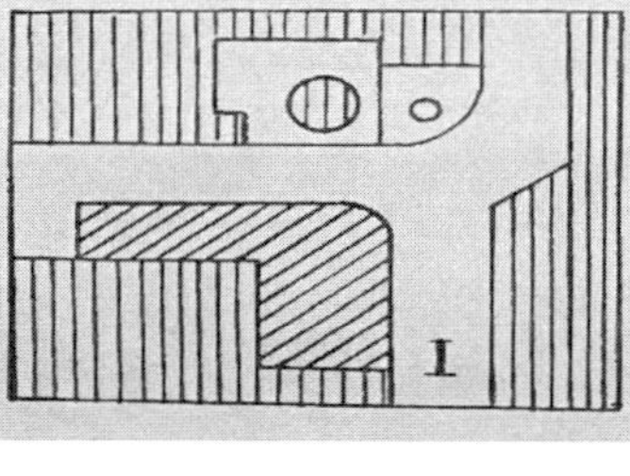

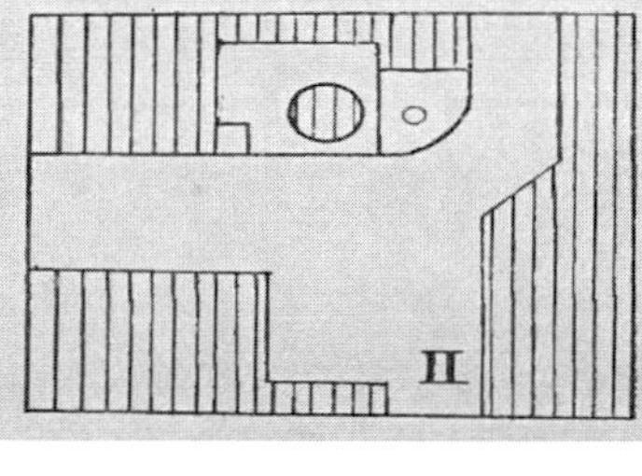

Town-Planning in Patiala State and City.

A REPORT

TO

H. H. THE MAHARAJA OF PATIALA

BY

PROFESSOR PATRICK GEDDES.

Member of the Town Planning Institute.

LUCKNOW:

PRINTED AT PERRY'S PRINTING PRESS.

1922.

Town-Planning in Patiala State and City.

CONTENTS.

PREFACE.

Regional Improvement and Development, Town-Planning and City Design,—as the writer has gradually come to see these through forty years and more of City study and endeavour—are tasks and problems much more complex than usually recognised by engineers, sanitarians and planners, or by those who consult and employ them.

The apparently simplest and most localised needs, and operations, of surgery have wider reactions, throughout the life and health of the patient, than was lately known. Hence even the oculist, or the dentist, looks deeper than did his predecessors ; he discerns, indeed relieves apparently remote bodily diseases: at times he even ministers to the mind within.

In social matters this is harder to see. Still, we are learning. Towards this, the writer's experience has compelled wider and deeper surveys, more cautious yet more thorough diagnoses, and thus treatment more comprehensive; yet also more moderate, even gentler, than is customarily applied. Thus the older heroic operations—still so frequent in would-be civic surgery—are here replaced by surgery more antiseptic in detail, and also conservative. The beginner soon amputates a damaged limb: but with more experience, he applies himself to mend and restore it to usefulness. With this later type of surgery goes a more developed nursing back to health. In this, good environment strengthens the body; and mental vigour, of hope and courage, is revived also. Mind helps to heal body, no less than body mind. So also for the body politic, the community—from home and group to village and town, even to City, Region and State. The improving environment is but the needed beginning of the re-nursing of damaged Place, diminished Work, depressed and discouraged Folk, back to efficiency in activity. The essential cure—this return towards social health and efficiency—requires the arousal and efforts, of all concerned, towards renewing themselves; and thence towards making their City what it may be, and thus should be.

The beginnings of this view are manifest in that ruling spirit of the material Arts—Architecture—which more or less inspires all planners. They appear too, in the recognition and use of Regional Survey, and City interpretation, towards appropriate treatment. But such organised science, even such organising Art, are but means of the community's Re-Education, in the fullest sense. And this towards its more effective Co-operation, towards the worthy ends of social life, which are temporarily obscured.

II.

Truest of all it is—as shown alike in the achievements and monuments of the historic Past, and by the failures and tragedies of the Present—that the bettering City of the Future needs renewal and development of vital idealisms—the souls of all its varied religions, whose applications, in life-guidance, have created what it most values.

Through the past fixation of these, or the present lapse, there have come about many of the evils from which the City suffers; and of which material decay, disease, poverty and more, are outward symptoms. Hence these evils are not really curable by material methods only: witness the many disappointments of would-be "Improvement Schemes".

In summary then, the needed treatment is first of all to put Heart into the community, the City. Say to revive this, since plainly but sleeping there; thus renewing the sense of Citizenship. Towards this, old separations may help instead of hinder. Family and Kinship, Caste and Group, with all their ties of tradition, may be roused to good-will; for which even old rivalries become generous, and incentive. Thus it is but a step from 'home-pride' to neighbourhood-feeling, helped by awakening "health-conscience". So too for efficiency in education; for productiveness, in Industry; and thus to true City pride, ennobling all, highest and humblest. To realise all this is the task before Citizenship. To lead this, is Civic Statesmanship. To evoke it, is a call to the Religions too.

That all this needs putting *Head* into the City is also manifest. It needs to think:—first to discern, and make conscious, all that is best in its Past. It needs to know its present—that is to survey its strange minglings of evils with good; and to interpret these—there nemesis, here hope. And it has then to mobilise skill and science towards remedies, and towards fresh progress, towards the Future. This Future too is seen as no distant Utopia. It is as definite as sowing and planting; as raising of crops, and of children, as these should be.

III.

Ideas thus aroused, and by Heart and Goodwill, there is no fear of *Hand*. Even the financial difficulties,—which obsess, often paralyse, the older types of City Improvement—are no longer alarming. For its essential Bank is not that of the small accumulations of the past, of the entangled obligations of the present—but the purpose of the Future. City Development is but the highest expression of that vigorous toil with which agriculture creates its harvests, or each new industry wins its new wealth; each working, year in, year out, with purpose. Had this purpose not existed in the past, there could have been no Cities. And though such effort has been slackened by many causes, its renewal is in progress. This our profession shows, of town-planning; now in renewal from antiquity. Indeed this renewal is even on wing, as City Design anew develops; and in East and West alike. In short then, to renew the City is the task of its Citizens: their Treasury has but to organise their energies, as their working out of approved plans proceeds.

IV.

How to arouse these energies?—is thus our problem. Intellectually, by a rationally schemed programme, large enough to awaken interest, even to stir imagination. Yet also moderate enough to be realisable within a few years effort, with growing result accordingly; and with some speedy results, as promise of more. Hence the present Report for Patiala, with its modest beginnings—as of cleansing, of whitewashing, of gardening and planting the town. Yet all this as no mere group of Garden Suburbs, much though these will have of health, well-being and beauty: but pointing also towards its fuller and finer development as Regional Capital; and this as Culture-City.

So too for Bhatinda :—Primarily a growing railway and business centre; yet with more and more of the finer sides of life as well. For these the best centres of commerce are increasingly finding practicable, even necessary.

IV.

Here to initiate this vital process, of City Renewal and Development, the vast sums too often dissipated by Cities, or by States, are not required—not even desired! The various Faiths do not thus hold their festivals, or maintain their activities, their educational endeavours, charities and the rest. They ask little beyond that moral support from Ruler, State and City which costs these little. So also here. Thus, an initial (and why not annual) Civic Festival, and Pageant,—much akin to those of Divali, Dussera, Moharram, etc.,—is here (as for Indian Cities especially) most important; alike for guiding the public, towards improvement and City development; and for arousing interest and sympathy, for evoking generous initiative, and wider participation. I speak from varied experience of the effects of such Festivals, both in East and West; and it is in fact my principal regret, on leaving Patiala, that this has not yet been possible. But I do not give up hopes of this, in other hands: indeed I plead for it, and as soon as may be.

V.

Here may be outlined a view of the possibilities of City Development in India. And particularly in the Native States, among which, besides considerable travel during the past eight years, I have now reported for seven; (as well as for many more Cities in as many of the leading British Provinces). And this also in comparison with long practice at home, in the capitals of the three Kingdoms, as also in France and Belgium, in Palestine, in Ceylon, and with repeated visits to America and other countries.

This varied experience has enabled me, (twice over), to accumulate the largest of collections of City Surveys, Plans, and other documents, illustrative of City Conditions and Improvements throughout the World.—Hence my Cities and Town-Planning Exhibition, which, after many wanderings through India and Europe, is now open in Bombay. Withs uch world-wide surveys in mind, I have the distinct impression—I am even been compelled to the reasoned view—that, though the possibilities of City Development are great in all lands there are at present, in the World, no opportunities more conspicuous, or more hopeful, than in the capitals and towns of the Native States of India.

For what reasons? Not simply because they have as yet often some leeway to make up—though that is often true, as even here. But for a larger reason. The world-history of City Development shows that this has only adequately taken place when the fertile union has occurred, of a deeply civilised and well-skilled people, ideally minded too—with an active individual leader—usually therefore their ruling Prince,—who has risen to the full height of his great position, with its comprehensive outlook and correspondingly wide appeal: and who has thus led and organised his people towards the civic achievements of peace, no less definitely as have others towards war. The supreme examples of the West are, in antiquity, Pericles for Athens, Augustus for Rome, and Solomon for Jerusalem—practically three Western Maharajas. The best later Cities tell the same tale. On one side that of a community with artistic qualities and technical skill; and with those deeper ideals, domestic, social, and cultural, which the Arts—and, above all, Architecture,—are needed to express—(and without which, Art falls to mere luxury and over-decoration, with social decline). Then for such communities the corresponding leadership—that of a Prince, rising from the comparatively simple and initial tasks of Palace-building, even Tomb or Temple-building, to City-building. Thus often throughout this monumental land, and splendid History, of India:—from Asoka to Akbar; or thence again to Man Singh of Jaipur, and many more.

It is this rare opportunity which lies here anew before the Indian Princes and their Cities: and thus in Patiala to-day. There are of course, dangers; in these pages later indicated—as from the Paris of Napoleon III, the Berlin of William I and II, and the like—of which there are also instances in India. For the ideal City can neither be built by Prince alone, nor by People alone. But by both together—since either alone is as an Army without a General, or a General without his Army with him.

VI.

It may be asked—on what grounds, this high estimate of the artistic, architectural, and deeper qualities of the people of this City? To this question two immediate answers may be given. First, that though Patiala is at first sight not to compare with the finer State Capitals through India, closer study, such as the writer has given during recent months, reveals a remarkable amount of domestic architecture of real beauty and this of local style, (as the accompanying sketches and water-colours show; though but samples, of what might have been multiplied tenfold).

It may again be said that this good, even beautiful, work is of the past, and too truly. The old mistris have been dying out, and with too few (when any) successors. But as proof positive that the true spirit, and even skill, of Architecture and of decoration still survives among the people and of this City, I need go no further back than to the recent Moharram. The "Tazzias" then carried in procession to the Karbala were necessarily few, and on modest scale, compared with those on like occasions in greater cities. They were also here produced by a section of the community inferior in numbers, wealth, and education to others. Yet I am bound to say that there were not a few which—alike as works of architectural design, and of beauty of decoration—I should be pleased and proud to exhibit in London, Paris, and other great Western Capitals of art and architecture. And I should do this with confident expectation that their current impression of the Arts of India, as in the main dying or dead, would be thereby transformed. Speaking with experience of the best work, and of picked workmen, of London, Edinburgh, Dublin, etc,—our leading cities—I am bound to say I could scarcely hope—or only with rarity—to elicit the like; and then at far greater expense.

Thus, even from these two local experiences out of many, I have no hesitation in squarely opposing,—with proof positive—the too common impression among my countrymen—even architects and artists who should know better—that the Arts of India are no longer deserving of encouragement. This idea also is disastrously prevalent among Indians themselves—Princes, Nobles, Ministers, and educated classes generally. It is thus most discouraging to the people,—to their mistris beyond all, since thus left too largely unemployed: or worse, displaced by the paper-educated draftsmen, of our hitherto mistaken system of education. In short, I am here with Mr. Havell, against all (too ill informed) pessimists.

I have thus no hesitation in maintaining, that this present moderate Programme of Improvement can be carried out in a very few years, without difficulty. Secondly, the present scheme may serve as a salient example, of the possibilities of the Native States and Capitals of India; wherever Prince and People are resolved to make the best of their present City, and towards its further development, when these leave it, as a worthy heritage to the succeeding generation.

VII.

The immediate business advantage of the present proposals is that they tend to the steady, and even speedy, improvement of City values. This whole scheme may be summed up, from the financial point of view, as corresponding to the re-appreciation of the real estate of that most extensive of family groupings which is a City, from its present depreciated condition.

Though no valuation is before us, it may readily be granted that a couple of crores would not pay for the house-property and sites of Patiala. But even at this moderate estimate, it makes a very great difference whether this value is to continue falling, as in the main it has too long been doing—or now to start effectively upon active rise of value. What other form of wealth-production can compare with this?—too little considered though it is by conventional economic teaching, or by business in individual competition.

And since this form of wealth-production has also immediate return (2) in health,—*i.e.*, in the quality—and duration—of life and pro-

ductive powers; as also on the other requirements of man—(3) in sociability, social order, harmony and progress—(4) in knowledge, education and thought—and (5) in the arts of life, with all their beauty and amenities as well as (6) in moral and religious values—such comprehensive range of improvement may fairly claim the consideration, and hope for active support accordingly, of all classes: in short from Prince and people, together.

P. G.

CHAPTER I.
Kandaghat

Here one cannot but appreciate the peculiarly fine and commanding situation with its convergent and crossing roads, each with wide and varied views. With such panoramic beauty of outlooks in all directions, great hopes naturally, and at once, arise for this development of a residential Hill-Station. Unfortunately however, as one proceeds with the quest of sites, these turn out to be fewer, and more difficult and costly of access, water-supply, etc , than could be at first sight anticipated.

After taking in the general lie and rise of the main hills and valleys, the position of the village with its old camping ground, and the situation of the various existing bungalows, etc., the first step towards fuller survey is naturally to go up the hill, beside the Station, past the Dispensary and the fine situation occupied by the house of the Diwan Sahib.

Beyond this a few other sites might be developed with facility of water-supply, though with increasing difficulty of access. So one naturally considers the possibility of a line of road above the railway, and as far as the bluff above its tunnel, which would admit here of a Zigzag descent to the main Simla Road. But such a road would be expensive, too much so for present likelihood of demand ; and so must be left to the future, with its possible increase.

This small climb however affords a good first view of the hill-group opposite ; and to this we now devote the day. We ascend by the line of the proposed road starting from Simla road beside the spring surrounded by trees, and winding upwards. Unfortunately the general slope is steep, and with few sites accordingly, till we reach the main ridge, with its fine outlooks in all directions. For clearer general view of the whole hill mass, and of the possible sites, yielded by its various descending ridges, we also ascend to the higher hill, that with small Gurdwara and Temple ; and make a further and final search for sites on the way down. But the result of the whole survey is disappointing. For though on the plan of the hill a good many sites at first seem promised, a closer study, alike of plan and actual contours, yields but few—one may safely say less, rather than more, than a score in all. This number will not repay the heavy expenses of road construction and of water-supply ; at any rate under present conditions. Moreover, despite the fine views, the soil is too thin and the shaly rock below does not retain water. The Bungalows would thus have both slow and poor success, alike with trees and gardens ; and the large initial outlays, for roads and water, would thus very slowly, if ever, produce any return upon this expenditure. I am deeply sorry therefore to be compelled to discourage these substantial outlays, rather than to advise them.

Still, an inexpensive and experimental beginning may be made, which can be carried further in the future, should sufficient demand arise. The little spring at the start of the proposed road may doubtless be somewhat improved, so as to yield water for at most a couple of bungalows, say one on each side, steep though these sides are. Given this local water, and the small section of road-making needed, these two bungalows may serve as a suggestive beginning.

Again along the Chail Road there are bluffs with fine views, especially down the river valley, but sufficiently above this to be free from the malaria mosquitos of the rice-fields deep below. Near the large Police Station compound also, several sites may be allotted. And finally further along the road, below the finely situated bungalow of H. H. the Maharaja, sites with gravitation water-supply may be noted.

If and when all or most of the above-mentioned sites are taken up, in the course of years, the development of the Central Hill-mass may more readily come up anew for consideration. Meantime something may be done towards holding up water upon these hills, beginning with the hollow immediately above the village camping ground, and utilising convenient situations above, by small rough dams easily constructed without much labour. This will encourage existing tree-growth, and admit of a little more planting and sowing of the common species of trees and shrubs hardy enough to grow upon the poor soil of these hills.

Towards the future development of Kandaghat one possibility may be suggested ; that of encouraging the start of one or two residential Boarding houses or Hotels, which would offer a pleasant change from the plains, and even from Simla also, especially in its times of cold and wet weather. Many hill-stations, and in all parts of the world, have been helped in this way.

Taradevi

Thus on the whole disappointed at Kandeghat, I take upon myself (though without instructions) to look into the possibilities of Taradevi. But here again the ridges are too steep, and very few sites can be discovered. The only fine area is that occupied by the Brick-field, and though this useful and doubtless remunerative enterprise should not be discontinued, its fairly large plateau area may be limited, so as to yield a few sites along its road (one easily capable of improvement); and also two or three on the remainder of the plateau, beyond the Brick-field. Finally the point above the turn of the Simla Road nearest the brick-field offers space for a single bungalow of magnificent view. And further back towards Taradevi, this narrow ridge expands, so as to yield a site or two more, though with steep access.

Close to Taradevi Station, the Plague Huts situation seems at first sight promising : but a road of access would be expensive. Hence, for the present at least, it will probably be more remunerative and useful to let these huts as cottages for labourers and foresters.

The hill-top encroachment of the large Dairy Enclosure near the station leaves an unsightly feature, and I therefore cannot but hope that this may be sold to the Dairy for its completion. Also very unsightly are the banks beside and around the Railway Station ; which latter is of awkward and unfinished accesses ; and I therefore submit that an amicable arrangement might readily be made for the simultaneous improvement of these blemishes upon this otherwise fine road and landscape by the State and the Railway Authorities, each for its own ground. Little spade work is required. The main improvement can be simply effected by sowing seeds of barberries and other common local shrubs on the bare places at the road side, and by planting acorns of the common local oak (Q. incana) upon the larger bare places of the forest hill-side, where quarrying has begun mischief, and denudation, even with landslips, have followed.

Jutog

Here we are almost at Simla, but between the Municipal Area and that of the big Cantonment Hill of Jutog, we are in Patiala. The ridge above the Jutog road is lying bare and waste, with only small ruins and a disused brick-kiln : but its east access and its magnificent view in both directions make this ridge perhaps the most attractive of all remaining situations for Bungalows (and perhaps even a Hotel,) in easy connection with the city. The railway boundary stones are here pushed back further upon the ridge than is usual ; and this seems explained by old quarrying operations, immediately above the railway, and which would obviously endanger it if resumed. If however these were filled up with uniform slope and planted, the railway might reasonably take back its boundary to the usual distance.

Not only may this range of ridge up to Jutog Station be thus profitably developed, but a further range of bungalows can be provided later, by making a road from a point below the Simla-Jutog Road, and to run below the Military area, at sufficient distance to yield bungalows both above and below its course, and without interference with the cultivated land of the neighbouring village, to which we thus also improve the access.

Summerhill

Just at the limit of Simla Municipality in this direction, a hill path runs on into the Patiala forest, which can be easily developed as a road. At first the slopes are steep, but a little further on they become easier with more bungalow sites accordingly. This area therefore may be naturally and profitably developed before many years.

Summary

The whole of these possible sites—from Taradevi to Summerhill—are therefore broadly indicated in colour upon the accompanying tracing of the map of Simla, and I trust may be profitably disposed of, in view of the scarcity of sites within Simla Municipal area.

May I point out, finally, that the old project of development, on Dehon Ghat Hill near Solen may be revived ; since practically all Solen sites are now occupied.

CHAPTER II.

Pinjaur

Location and Interest.

Of all the various planning opportunities of Patiala State, none can be more attractive than Pinjaur to an old gardener like the writer, with lifelong experience of the great gardens of Europe, and some past responsibilities amid those of India, up to that of the Taj Mahal itself. For here is one of the best preserved of all the magnificent Moghal gardens; and hence the one most readily recoverable from forest overgrowth to its ancient and ordered beauty. Here too one clearly sees how just are the appreciations of this style of gardening by Mr. Havell* and Mrs. Villiers Stuart,† of which the latter's vivid and charming description of Pinjaur will be found interesting and helpful to every visitor.

Assuming then these general appreciations of the style, and this particular appreciation of its feature and results at Pinjaur, the present task is of offering suggestions as to (1) how such restoration and reclamation as has been in the main fairly well done in the smaller and upper garden may be continued; and (2) how similar conservative improvement may be extended to the lower garden gradually, and with most economy of labour and yet resultant effect, and even useful return.

Given water and soil, the great question is of labour. The Chief Mali tells me he has 25 men already fully occupied; and to my question of how many he will need if the whole garden is to be kept in order, he replies "25 more at least".

I do not say this rough estimate is wrong; under present conditions indeed it seems as reasonable as may be. But first I recall my ramble through the little town of Pinjaur, now reduced to 500 inhabitants from what may well have been 5,000, as its vast extent of ruins shows; and of the local doctor's malancholy record, of treating no less than 4,000 fever cases last year in Pinjaur and neighbourhood; as also his unfavourable report upon the bulk of the local water-supply, as conducive to rheumatism and other ailments, even goitre itself. Under these circumstances labour cannot but be much below normal efficiency: and if so, the sanitary improvement of the town becomes "a business proposition", preceding the effective treatment of the garden; as of course also for rendering the palace and garden themselves healthy, instead of too fully sharing, as they have so long done, in the malarial conditions and dangers of their neighbourhood.

In this regard, I next bethink me of the finest private garden in Europe, the late Sir Thomas Hanbury's fine old 'Palazzo Orengo' at Ventimiglia, just over the Franco-Italian frontier from Mentone, and

---

* A V Havell—The Taj Mahal

† C M Villiers Stuart—Gardens of the Great Moghals London 1913

not only the great "sight" of that region, but a centre of pilgrimage for botanists and gardeners from all countries. Here I have once and again lived and studied; and I well remember that my host took pleasure and legitimate pride, in explaining how at the very outset of his great design of reclamation and planting, which has year by year employed from 60 to 80 or 100 gardeners, he saw it a necessity and found it a pleasure, first of all to put his whole village in sanitary order, and thereafter to keep it so. Palace and village thus form one healthy community, alike well housed and brightly gardened, in their respectively magnificent and modest ways, and each effectively helpful to the other. So largely throughout Britain, where the great noble, with his castle or palace, his vast park and gardens, is also proud to show his guests the order and beauty of his village outside his gates.

Pinjaur is no ordinary village, but a place of classic and religious interest, and even of pilgrimage to its famous Spring and sacred Bath. Not only do its many temples and tanks, and its large old mosque, give it a monumental character; easily enhanced by clearance of ruins; but its wealth of ancient carved stones, and these often of singular beauty, invite a careful Archæological Survey, and promise rich return to even moderate surface excavations. I venture therefore to plead for an invitation to the Archæological Department at Simla, to send down one of their skilled and learned investigators, whose experience might readily and inexpensively yield a rich harvest, and this not only of artistic treasures, but even of light upon this classic region; if not from the Pandava heroes of the Mahabharata, at least of its subsequent history, so long inspired by memories of these.

Proposed Rides

The great walls of this whole garden, upper and lower together, measure nearly a furlong over a mile. Their aspect is too plain and featureless to have much character within; but outside they are higher, and offer each along a magnificently picturesque perspective, thanks to the octagonal Burj at each corner, the gate-way on each side, and the fine semi-circular buttress-towers between. Since fifty yards beyond the walls is also palace property, (only in part encroached on by village cultivators), I propose here a Circuit Ride. Not of course a formal road, but a simple grass ride, so much pleasanter and less costly while serviceable also for pasture, and kept in order by this. A line of trees can readily be planted along its outer border,—say mulberries on one side of the garden, plants on the other, and cypresses along the foot. This one-sided treatment seems preferable to a full avenue, since not obscuring the three long monumental perspectives of castellated walls. But if a complete avenue be preferred there is still room to plant the inner row of this—say a hundred, at least ninety, feet from the walls—without too much obscuring the view of them.

Furthermore, though the interior garden is terraced, there are easy slopes next the wall within, so that an inside ride next the walls is also easily practicable. The gates on three sides of this larger garden are closed up; but easily re-opened, thus affording fully six furlongs more of grass ride, and varied combination with the outer ride also.

I am aware that complete privacy for this lower garden is at times desired; but when the main central view,—that from the palace arcade-hall and down the main water-course, and its terraces to the bottom gate—is carefully studied, it will be seen how much this view would gain were this gate-way re-opened as a central focus of light, instead of a blot of darkness. I therefore plead for the re-placement of the rough brick wall which at present closes up each gate by simple folding gates, of light wrought-iron tracery: with these backed with light wooden doors, to be closed when desired. The dull interior walls can be readily brightened by flowering creepers; and at intervals a wired-in space along the walls, narrow, but of long flight, will give the best and simplest of aviaries.

Continuation of this Ride

With only a little clearing through and around the ruined streets of Pinjaur, this ride may next loop round and through the town, winding its way across the brooks and past the monuments. A fine beginning of the proposed grass ride, and one indicating the proposed connection between palace and village, is already available along the brook to northwards of the main entrance bridge. The neighbouring ugly modern cook-house-block, and the little square Water-control-house are easily veiled in creepers: and the little mud and thatched cottage, with its coloured front, is well worth preserving.

Main Entrance

The short avenue from the public road is in very poor order, and will reward some planting and care. The ugly brick-work just before reaching the entrance gate posts may be covered with a creeper, as also these two modern posts themselves. The unsightly twistings upon the entrance drives within—badly exaggerated from European drives—should be straightened, still leaving ample thoroughfares, but now of the more formal character the architectural style requires. The iron verandah and European greenhouse criticised by Mrs. Villiers Stuart have happily been removed: but the unnecessary rubbish heaps, to the south of the entrance gateway should of course also disappear. May not the stream be here held up into permanent pools, which would give a fine little river landscape? Mosquito pools would thus be abolished; and fish would keep the water clean, while its seepage would help this entrance lawn and its trees, even appreciably the garden within as well.

The fine yellow-stemmed bamboo clumps may be multiplied beside the stream on both sides, and with advantage.

Economic Trees

Among the interesting trees upon the entrance lawn let me specially call attention to the two young carobs (Ceratonia siliqua)

Further plants should be obtained; since this tree, like the date, is of separate sexes, which must be grown together for fruit. But if this be produced and in possible quantity, it will next pay richly to obtain grafts from the Mediterranean (especially from Cyprus, which has the best variety), since no better cattle-food exists; and palatable and wholesome for man as well. This tree has moreover, in high degree, the quality of enriching soil, not only by the fall of its thick leafage, but by its ample root-tubercles, providing nitrogenous manure for the crops which are grown below. If then the carob succeeds here, a great and profitable co-operation is possible between forester and agriculturist throughout this region.

In this economic connection let me also call attention to the kindred hopes raised by the recent introduction of the best Arabian date-trees, and the best varieties of Smyrna figs, which are due to the enterprise of Mr. Milne, Government Botanist and Principal of the Agricultural College at Lyallpur. For just as within the Pinjaur garden, we find the very best of mangoes, yet these growing side by side with the very poorest, so may we not hope for a similar contrast of the varieties of other fruits ?

Finally the fine growth of mulberry trees at Pinjaur raises further economic hopes: not merely of silk, but even more of fodder—and why not perhaps even of ensilage ?

Entrance Gate and Garden

This entrance garden fortunately retains a good deal of the stately and formal character of its old design. This however should be more completely recovered. The few surviving Cypresses indicate the original design, and their rows should therefore be completed; with cutting out of other trees as the Cypresses rise. Outside these again the palm lines should be completed; even with the labour of setting back the existing border of shrubbery, (Hibiscus, Acalypha, Russellia, &c. to which Jasmines, Roses, &c, may be added).

The map of 1877-8 shows the two halves of this entrance garden each sub-divided into four small squares by intersecting paths; but these have been removed and the whole thrown into path areas, by some gardener of the then prevalent English taste. It is worth considering whether these minor paths should not be reinstated; and not merely as restoring the original design, for piety's sake, but for the effective contrast which this gave with the two large open squares of the next section of the garden immediately below.

On the other hand the fine purple masses of the Bougainvillea climber are an addition which the original designers would have welcomed; and these are well worth leading more profusely along the interior of the entrance wall. The more general adornment of the two blank walls of this whole garden by means of varied climbers is also here well worth considering; since no other plants yield such brilliant result, or with less attention.

Inner Garden

We now descend to this lower level by either of the small stairways on each side of the picturesquely designed Shish Mahal. Here again the straight canal has so far compelled preservation of the formal design, not only in its jasmine bordering, but in its row of palms. This however may with advantage be continued one tree further. There is also just enough room for planting an additional row parallel to this. The walk on each side may be narrowed with advantage by a yard (upon its outer side from the canal), thus increasing its apparent length. A row of cypresses, parallel to the palms, can thus be planted, with roses between; and a bright border of shrubbery may still shut off the open lawns on either hand.

The terrace wall separating this inner (Palace) garden from the Entrance Garden above is at present ineffectively bordered; merely with a low-growing Euphorbia, with its small red flowers. Here should be planted a line of exuberantly coloured shrubs; say argwan (Bauhinia) in its red and yellow and variegated varieties, and also some vigorous creepers, (Bignonia, &c.) to swing along low posts and chains, on top of the terrace wall above, and thus also adorn its upper Walk.

Enlargement of the Palace

This is manifestly necessary, since the present building has too small accommodation. Yet enlargement needs to be done with the greatest care, in fact with the utmost moderation, since the original design has already given it just the right magnitude, proportions and height. The increase of this palace in the ordinary way, by lofty wings, would thus ruin the present effect, of a great garden and a moderate palace; since a great palace would inevitably overpower the garden, and make it look comparatively small. Nor can the small Shish Mahal above be enlarged without disastrous loss of its present charming proportions and effect.

Since however the additional accommodation required is after all not great, a row of one-storey rooms can be added along the southward side, with verandah corridor in front *i. e.*, to eastward; and also with a fine broad verandah platform overlooking the great garden below, and based on pillars rising from the existing low buttresses which strengthen the main wall. This extension enables the adjacent Indian Guest House (formerly Forest Office) to be taken into the Palace Extension, if required. This building can also be extended, if necessary, upon its wall.

Possible Further Extension

If further extension be required, a similar one-storey wing may connect up the present palace with the European Guest House on the northward. Only here it is most neccessary to avoid spoiling the effect of the one fine piece of interior garden wall—that with the rounded buttresses and shield-shaped battlements—by raising anything above their line; for (as will be seen from the lower garden), the extension of the one-storey level of the Guest House would rise above this, and with thoroughly bad effect.

The way to avoid this is however easy; that of sinking these new rooms, between Palace and Guest House by four or five feet. This can easily be done by slightly narrowing the present Walk to the Guest House; and giving it a small terrace slope down to the verandah pillars of these few new rooms. With this terrace slope grassed, and planted with bulbs, the interior effect would also be pleasing.

If and when either or both of these present Guest Houses are thus absorbed into the palace, it will be easy and inexpensive to supply similar one-storey buildings further up the north and south wall; conveniently just below the terrace of the upper Entrance Garden.

Though time has not permitted measurement for exact plans, the whole scheme prepared will be readily understood from the accompanying sketches.

CHAPTER III.

Pinjaur Lower Garden

This whole garden was obviously designed to be viewed from the open hall of the Palace : and this manifestly as a whole ; spreading on each side of its main central perspective of its Canal and spacious Baradari Basin, into its fourfold ranges, each of four Garden-squares ; and with their broad intermediate Walks widening at their crossing into platformed squares, three on each side, and one at bottom.

Now of this view too little remains. Only the first four squares, those immediately below the palace, can plainly be seen ; for beyond these there is now substantially on either hand only a mango forest. Of this the trees also intrude too far upon the central canal line, concealing the Baradari and its great square pool, and too much shutting up the distant landscape, of which only a peep remains.

Yet alteration must be gradually proceeded with ; and this at once for economy's sake, and for beauty of effect, since the forest growth has also its charm, which sudden and sweeping felling would destroy. The renewed effect of the old design must therefore be recovered more gradually, throughout a term of years. So towards this a careful study has been made, of every square, walk, and widened crossing, as well as of the central view.

Central Perspective

Here a creditable, though incomplete, beginning has been made towards restoration. The line of small palms along the canal borders furnish the main feature of this, though with too frequent gaps, which should of course be filled up, and with as tall plants as possible. The line of jasmines between should also be more fully enriched, by alternating roses, etc. The small wire arches, from English suburban gardens, are here too weak and slight for effect, and thus had better be removed; but their climbers may be grown horizontally along the side of little bridges which cross the canal at intervals (by simply turning a wire for their support between the low arches of each bridge).

Over the canal wall of each side the existing trees spread too freely, each thus contributing to close the view. It will mostly suffice however at first to remove the smaller trees, as notably the loquats, and thus make room for replanting the row of cypresses which were certainly of the original design, since alone keeping regular outline, without closing up the perspective, as even large palm heads cannot but do. Where a mango however comes in the way, it should be sacrificed; but in other cases its branches may be carefully pruned back, so as to open the view, without leaving the tree looking maimed and unsightly. The Malis in this garden, as in others throughout India, are apt to spoil the trees they lop; so that this work should be done by a good forester and under the supervision of the ranger, at least until some Mali can be trained to do it as well. The three existing Eucalyptuses should be pruned of branches which obscure the view, but may be left until their beauty begins to pass, as it will in a few years.

The second section of the canal needs similar treatment to the first, with its existing palm row completed round the whole Baradari Tank Square. The Cypress border on each side of the Canal walk should similarly be completed; indeed this time in double row on each side, though single around the Tank-Walk Square.

The disuse of Cypresses in Indian gardens is not a little explained by the common recent English prejudice against them as funereal, and which relegates them to cemeteries accordingly. But the great Italian gardens have none of this prejudice, and obtain their main effect with Cypresses accordingly. Best of all, the old Moghal and Hindu gardeners, as all old garden pictures show, used the cypress as a symbol of life and immortality; and they wreathed it for joy, with festoons of roses and climbers, or often planted alternating fruit trees. It is of course this appropriate tradition and treatment that needs to be recovered here.

Beside the Baradari Tank there are happily distinct survivals of this old treatment; as notably in the long borders spreading north and south at right angles to the course of the main canal. For here are cypresses alternating with oranges and with roses; so the completion of the old design is as natural and easy as it will be pleasing.

The third section of the canal, below the Baradari Tank, is thickly and closely grown with big mangoes. Though their fruit is scanty and poor, one regrets cutting them; yet the main perspective will too soon be closed up altogether unless their front row be sacrificed, for the more orderly cypresses which should replace them.

Along the fourth and lowest section of the Canal—which has most but not all its lines of palms, and a walk border of beautiful crape-flower bushes (Lagerstrœmia) there are few large trees, and these not worth retaining so that here a concluding double row of cypresses on each side should be planted. It will be remembered that a double row is also above recommended for the second canal level; so that there will thus be an alternation of single and double cypress rows, thus avoiding monotony of line. Finally, to complete the series and perspective, a single cypress tree should be planted in line, just outside the gate at the very bottom of the garden. Here a wrought-iron gate, affording a focal point of light, seen as brighter in the deep shadow of the gateway arch, may again be recommended as above (page 6) to complete this long perspective from the Palace arcade hall.

Treatment of Garden Squares, and Walks.

The first two central squares, immediately below the palace, are at present practically each in open park, with only few and scattered trees, and may substantially remain so, since this well-watered grass keeps green throughout the year. The small oranges planted in the southerly square should be thinned, and narcissus, tulip, and other bulbs may be planted in the grass. The upper walk, immediately below the palace wall, may be bordered with low palms and perfume-giving shrubs (jasmines, etc.) along its length, and thereafter (beyond the present Guest Houses) with higher growing climbers on the wall, and larger fragrant flowering trees upon the opposite side say the Champak (Michelia Champaka) and the other Champak or pagoda-tree (Plumeria acutifolia).

On the remaining three sides of each of these two front squares, low growing palms will furnish effective avenue borders, alternating with decorative and fragrant bushes, like Carandas, &c., and of course not forgetting roses and jasmines, &c. Immediately below the first terrace, hidden by a big mango and other trees one finds an immense Champak (Plumeria) with twisted old stems, probably the most certain survivor of the first planting of the garden, and still surprisingly rich in leafage and even flowers. This well deserves release and recovery from the mangoes which crowd it in. Beside it there is also the other Champak (Michelia) which may also be spared for its fragrant blossom. The interior of this lower square is a long neglected, but not unbeautiful, thicket of pomegranates. That on the other side of the canal has oranges, but in much worse condition. Their improvement (or more probably replacement) can be gradually done without any unpleasant period of blankness.

The third pair of central squares are still more in wilderness: on the south side with pomegranates among mangoes, and on the north mangoes with a few oranges; but none apparently of value.

The fourth pair of squares are in wilderness yet more complete; with a few very old mangoes, perhaps dating from the original planting, so that the best may be preserved till death begins, as it is doing with several already, which may be cut down with advantage.

Finally, the four squares to north and south of these along the garden walls are yet more neglected: those towards the west in densest wilderness, those towards the east more spare, but long neglected too. What then can best be done, with space so large; and without undue expense?—indeed if possible, as a garden should be, with useful and profitable return? And yet all in the tradition of the place, as far as may be; or at most with such development of it as its original makers and planters could approve, could they return?

We may at any rate be fairly sure that they, as not only artist-designers and master-builders, but fruit-growers as well as flower-lovers, would fully appreciate the striking contrast between their familiar old mangoes of the lower garden and the large and luscious fruits of the upper; and would enquire into their origin and their grafting. And would they not need ask.—Why then not more of these? And why not the like for other fruit? Oranges? Pomegranates? Guavas? Dates? Figs? and so on. So with the finer roses, the occasional unfamiliar shrubs and flowers. Thus we moderns may rest assured that so long as we recover and renew, yet preserve, the old tradition of this great garden of the past they are fully with us, and we with them, in developing this heritage as a centre of finer culture of all kinds; and thus not only of trees and fruit-trees, of shrubs and flowers, but even of the homely vegetables which they must have also had place for.

In this way the policy of improvement yet with continuity and progress yet with order, is seen to apply to a garden as to a state: and the historic love and care of gardens by so many of the great rulers of the past, and this in all countries and civilisations, is thus better understood. Year by year they practised on the small scale what they sought to accomplish on the great; and thus they returned, refreshed in mind and soul as well as invigorated in body, to apply in the conduct of their peoples' life what they had learned from watching and guiding the varied growth of nature.

At once then loyal to tradition, yet open to progress, we may go through this great garden once more, re-calling, conserving its significance from the earliest past, as from its central and cosmic crossing, originally, as older gardens show, the four Rivers of Paradise. Yet also in practical spirit, and this invigorated, not weakened, much less sentimentalised.

First of all then, the Palace needs not only flowers and fruits, but vegetables; and only western snobbery, not Indian feeling, can oppose growing them here. So where most naturally and conveniently? Next the cook-house, of course; *i. e.* in the two squares to the north-east. In the upper, the best of vegetables; in the lower the ordinary ones of the district. For here at once we have the same educative object-lesson as with the mangoes wild and perfected; the same contrast between the tiny potatoes of the every day market, and the big fine ones from Scottish or other best seed; and similarly for peas, beans, tomatoes and all the rest. Here then are two garden squares, each in order; not only useful but also of educative interest to people and palace, to mali and to Prince alike; since full of suggestions of improvements, not only bearing on local well-being, but gradually spreading suggestion and imitation throughout the State, and beyond. The introduction of the potato may be justly enough credited to Sir Walter Raleigh; but it was not until five generations later that it came widely into use, and then not until the King of France came to the rescue, and overcame prejudice by growing them in his own garden, nominally for himself, but really for his villagers, who soon were curious to try their King's strange new "earth-fruit".

But curiosity is the spring of science; of practical progress largely too. So let the next lower square (the third down the northern wall) be open to all plants of interest and wonder to man, the familiar and the strange alike, the useful and the medicinal—in fact a little Botanic Garden, of which the charm and wonder will increase, Here for instance Bose's sensitive plants, and others he has made world-marvels: here too of course, Darwin's wonders of flower-fertilisation; and so on throughout the paradise of science; and through the varied magic of healing too.

The bottom square, and its neighbour southwards, are alike mere jungles. In each of these a sturdy forest-squad may be set for a week to clear, sparing only the few fine or ancient trees. Then speedily they can replant with a Fruit-orchard and a Forest-nursery for result; and these each with its own interest and value, its stimulus throughout the region again as well. Here then is this northern range of long neglected squares, redeemed from deterioration into jungle, and each more interesting than another, each most valuable in its own way. Thus in the upper squares, the gardening of the people, and of domestic needs for the palace; in those three lower ones, the more advanced and scientific cultures those for science and medicine, of fruitgrowing and forestry. What now of the next three? those to south-west?. Here, most of all, wild nature has returned, in wild forest and jungle, where not only the wild peafowl nest, but the panther pounces on them. For the present then, till all else is in order, let us leave these squares wild. Yet not unhumanised; for here in the forest has ever been the retreat of the religious and meditative spirit. Here too the more recent quests of science, eager to learn the ways of nature from tree to weed, from birdnest to anthill. Here too the poet has ever refreshed his inspiration by return to nature: while all three together—the spiritual, the intellectual, the imaginative—are ever telling, to us of the busy world, that their secrets may be best learned from nature, and for ourselves.

This appreciation and preservation of wild nature does not preclude appropriate improvement as time and garden-resources allow. The space of religion may be bordered with the flowers most sacred to the memories and meditations of all the faiths, and centred around a pipal or a banyan. In that of observant science fresh seeds may be scattered, alike from near and far; and around that of imagination may be planted the flowers of the poets, the bulbs of spring, the perfumed blossoms of Indian and Persian song, and of antique book-illumination and painting.

Further Design and Philosophy of the Garden.

We have thus gone round most of the outer squares, those outside the four central ones round the Baradari Tank; and before completing the series let us return for a moment to the central Baradari itself. For what purpose this ? Obviously for pleasure at its fullest, beyond even the Palace, from which it is the main retreat for coolness amid its waters, deep enough, and inviting, for the bath and swim. A place too for music and song, for society, conversation and story-telling, for fruit feasting and *sherbat* drinking ; yet also at times for council, for solitary thought as well. What might not such thought at times see, ranging over the four surrounding fruitful and flowery squares, the four long perspectives up down and across, between the twelve outer squares, and up to the Palace, down to the landscape beyond ? Neither the Moslem makers of this garden, nor its Sikh conquerors, nor we European admirers and students of it, have accepted the Hindu caste-system with its rigidity : yet it is in the very essence of all our forms of social life, and now for a hundred years the basal thought of social science, that human life and order are most broadly intelligible as fourfold. First, since most fundamentally and simply, the life of the people, in their every-day place and work ; thus conditioning their ways, as different types of folk. Next the life of their immediate and managing superiors, with wider knowledge of places, fuller experience of work, and thus efficiency for its business-like direction ; a more understanding grasp, practical accordingly, of the people's ways, their morals and manners, their customs and laws, with management and direction accordingly. Here then is the old meaning of Manu's divisions of peasant cultivators as Sudras, of the business world as Vaishyas ; and though as non-Hindus, we do not use these names, we cannot but maintain their underlying elements of fact. Again what of Manu's third caste, of Brahmins ? However little we accept their concrete claims, their abstract ones are universally human ; for these proclaim the world of religious and mystic emotion, deepened from the simple feeling of the every-day labouring and business world which we (as they) have passed in review. Here then is the world of the intellectual life, whether more philosophic with the Hindu, more scientific with Western, or mathematical with both. And here also the imaginative life, whether its poetry be mythologic with the Hindu, lyric with the Persian or dramatic in the West. The people and their practical chiefs are alike absorbed in their every-day life, the first content in place, and work and folk, the latter with more developed sense-observation, with work-experience as skill in affairs, and with folk-feeling developed to guidance and direction. They thus constitute what history and social science call the 'Temporal Power.' But emotion, intellect and imagination, religion, philosophy and science, poetry and symbolism are ever building up the Spiritual Power : and this is less apart from the simpler preceding life than they have generally realised, since now sociology and psychology are proving its constant evolution from this.

"People" and "Chiefs" as "Temporal Power" are thus so far balanced by these "Intellectuals," with each and all of their three-sided activities. But with these the Spiritual Power is still incomplete. Thought, though fundamentally passive, and so far withdrawn from every-day life and experience, ever also tends to complete itself in social action. The moral and religious life ever returns to its community, its polity; and seeks to reshape this as Etho-polity. Thus Philosophy is no mere abstract culture of old, nor is science to-day; their abstract thought must realise itself as social wisdom, and counsel, for the Etho-polity, *i e.* the community in its highest aspect. Thus intellectual reflection yields not merely "pure science," but it is ever seeking to realise itself also in deed. But in what manner of deed? Here is the field of the purified and developed imagination; by which the noblest poetry of each and every people has indeed sung of the deeds and heroes of the past, but also to nerve the man of the present to fresh achievement. Etho-polity in wisdom, organisation towards achievement—here arises the culmination of the spiritual power, since reshaping, revitalising the temporal also. Here then the general process of all great civilizations, those of the East and of the West alike. Manu's teaching was thus fulfilled in ancient Hindu Rule at its greatest; so too Buddha's and Asoka's; so again Mohammed's, and more, in Akbar's; and so again with the great Sikhs, gurus and leaders by turns.

Since philosophy is the generalising of man's work and experience by his thought, it is plain that the above interpretation has also largely arisen from previous planning detailed above (page 12-13) of the outer garden squares. First for horticulture with the People; then for botany, fruit growing and forestry with their skilled and working Chiefs, next for religion, science and poetry with the Intellectuals; and now finally for etho-polity, wisdom organisation, and achievement, as the culminating series, for the Expressionals—and these, in India of all countries, have ever been Princes and Rulers at their best.

It is thus by no mere accident that vast and symbolically ordered gardens like this one have only been made by men of this highest responsibility; and when not sovereigns then grand viziers, like Fadai Khan here. It is not by mere possession of wealth: were that all, the great bankers, the great industrialists could make them; but this they have never yet done.

That gardens like these were made for rest, for recreation, for active pleasure, is of course clear throughout their whole design and adornment, is of course true; and not forgotten in the preceding pages; but they also have their very highest value and significance in their vast perspectives. Clear views for the outward eye are ever evoking clear views for the inward eye also. Do we not thus better understand the historic fact that these great Moghals carried on their Empire-making and their Garden-making together,—and did not both powers ebb together as well? Such gardens were thus not simply sanatoria, pleasure-retreats, hunting lodges, hospitality centres, and the rest ; though all these, of course ; these sovereigns and statesmen also made and used them for their hours of reflection and meditation, their times of council and counsel, their long plannings towards organisation and success, their moments of decision towards achievement. Their garden in fact was their university, and more ; for the statesman's university is his world: and from the earliest planning of cosmic cross and four rivers, and onwards through varied symbolisms to the more modern (yet also ancient) interpretation outlined above, such gardens have ever been microcosms of the great world.

Let this old gardener, the present writer, then ask his hospitable Prince to walk round the garden with this interpretation of it ; yet not as he has described and proposed to improve it, in his working way from north-east backwards, but now the right hand way, "*pradakshina*." First then the three great squares of the eastward angle here interpreted as for Etho-polity, Wisdom-organisation, and Achievement: and it is for him to choose out of the rich varieties of garden-resources how he will best symbolise these. But if suggestion be invited, what of centering the first of these with the old Tirbani, the three-fold tree-planting symbolic of his three-fold people ?—and with pomegranates, so full of flower and fruit and seed, around their grouping. And for the third square, of Achievement, what more appropriate through history, than the "golden apples" of so many legendary and heroic quests ?—yet not forgetting, with these glorious oranges, the citrons of sharper flavour.

Descending the garden, princes have ever listened to the poet's song ; and sometimes, though perhaps too seldom, shared the intellectual's quest : but it has been best with them when they entered at times the retreat of the religious, and learned from them to bow before the deeper mysteries of the universe and the higher laws that nature and humanity conceal and yet reveal.

Now leaving this triad of the intellectuals, and recalling sovereignty, with the passing view of the palace above, the square is reached of the most statesmanlike of all non-governing occupations, and indeed the most foresighted of any ; that of forestry, with its briefest planting plans for a decade, its longer plans for a generation, its further plans for four and five of these ; and thus, in time for the reclamation and enrichment of a half-ruined India, indeed a more than half-ruined world, by due afforestation once more. Beyond this, the speedier return of fruit trees—domestic forestry in fact—with its immense possibilities for the health and wealth not only for this favoured region but towards the hills above, the plains below. Then comes the botanic and medical garden, with its still not half-explored possibilities ; and so concludes the triad of gardens of special knowledge and technical skill.

Now the final triad : first that of every day popular gardening ; laborious, but poor in its common varieties of plants, its unskilled manuring, its shallow cultivation, and so on : and then beyond this, in dramatic contrast, the garden of full horticultural skill, with its fourfold or even manifold yield, and of better, more nutritious, more palatable, crops. Finally, right below the Palace Arcade up to and beside the squares for Etho-polity, comes the square of the Folk, with its appropriate framing as of Tulsi-border for Hindus, palm-border for the Moslems, and spreading shisham for the Sikh people and their dynasty. For as there is a time and a place for everything, surely therefore for the children to approach their father, the people their Prince.

A Greek Interpretation of the Garden.

But now the reader may well be weary: and complaining that this gardener-botanist is giving too much of his social philosophy, and this too grave and serious for a garden of pleasure. Yet the cure of the grave side of philosophy is the gay: and here also in this garden it is plain for all to see. For as Indian thought claims to have stirred and aroused that of the Greeks, so Indians were far too intelligent not also to be interested in the Greek thought, which more than Alexander's campaigns brought them. Brightest and highest of all these Greek thoughts, beyond even their splendidly human gods, the Olympians, was that of the inner divinities of the human spirit, the Nine Muses; yet these also vividly realised and embodied even to their ninefold hill-side garden, much as here upon the mountain slope, and, again like this, watered from an inspiringly sacred spring. Without positively claiming definite Greek origin for these nine spacious crossings of the broad-walks of this sixteenfold garden (and around the four squares of the Baradari Tank and at its centre) one may safely claim that the general unity of the human spirit (and not merely its geometry) may locate them here as well, indeed must do so, in fact has done so. First Erato, muse of simple human love, yet sublimatory into all higher love, of kindred and people, race and humanity. Her place therefore is at the central crossing below the palace, as common to prince and people, and both together. On the people's side is the muse of Dance and simple rhythm, from which all art-music comes, whom the Greeks called Terpsichore: and on the prince's side the Epic Muse, singer of great careers, Calliope. Next on the Baradari Tank level, on the people's side the spirit of folk-song, and art, the Lyric Muse, Euterpe. And on the Prince's side, Urania her of achievement in the great world; yet this, be it noted, in peaceful agriculture and architecture rather than in War. Again above the lowest terrace-level, amidst the usefully and skilfully designed squares of science, fruit-growing, forestry, is the Muse of Success, with her reward of triumph over the difficulties of life turned to opportunities,—Thalia, the Muse of Comedy. The opposite crossing, between the squares of the intellectuals, is obviously that of Polyhymnia, so called because so numerous are the philosophies and the sciences, so varied their poems. Between these and the last crossing and descent of the life stream, stands the grave muse Melpomene, the Tragedy with which life ends. Yet this ennobled, as Sacrifice. And finally—at the very centre, the Baradari platform,—all these eight Muses meet, and sing their tales to the ninth, Clio, the Muse of History, by whom the songs and stories of the past are kept in memory, and who thus is ever gathering the new.

Where better should we look for, and where more naturally find, these Nine Muses, than here at Pinjaur, by this old spring of the Heroes?—than in this old garden made by a past imperial Statesman?—or in this renewing garden, of a manly, strenuous, and purposive Prince?

CHAPTER IV.

Patiala City.

(Introductory) Rival Methods of City Improvement "Metropolitan" and "Civil."

A:—THE METROPOLITAN SCHOOL.

The method of would-be city improvement still most common in Indian capitals, as formerly in European ones, since its fashion was set by Napoleon III for Paris (1854-70) may naturally be termed the Metropolitan school. Its results are magnificent as regards perspectives, especially to and from the Palaces and public buildings, in connection with which these were naturally designed, as also for carriage traffic, and for military march and ride. Berlin naturally followed suit, as the capital of the German Empire after 1871, though with less artistic result. English utilitarianism, though impressed, even more or less dominated, by this school, had naturally to introduce its own ideas and phrases: and these are still only too prevalent throughout India. Hence, for instance "Sanitation", though too much under the facile and self-deceptive phrase of "reducing congestion in overcrowded areas", as of course also of "facilitating business communications"; and all naturally with cheering promises and best intentions of rehousing the people evicted for demolition, and this better than before. Yet this planning failed to grasp the economic conditions; *e. g.* of retail trade, or those of poorer middle class, working class, and labourers' housing; and thus it concentrated on making new and wide communications; and necessarily through the old-fashioned quarters occupied by these. And since one at first only thinks for the life and work within his experience, and in terms of the class he is identified with, this planning has been essentially towards "getting through" these congested quarters, and too little towards improving the trading or living in them.

Sweeping clearances are thus effected by the energies of engineers and demolition contractors; and an ever-increasing official staff and business connection, and a favourable press also, naturally encourage Improvement authorities to extend and multiply these.

But all these clearances have to be paid for; and improvements are expected to pay their way, at least in aggregate, and as soon as possible. Compensations for buildings demolished are naturally estimated at current values, and such properties are more or less depreciated; but an additional 10 or 15 per cent. of compensation for disturbance is given; and this appears liberal, or at any rate fair and sufficient, as it intends to be. Unfortunately however, this total compensation is seldom sufficient for reconstruction on the required scale: moreover, the recipient has only too often to apply this cash to meet other claims: so practically but little of the destroyed class of property is replaced by its evicted owners; and their housing difficulty, and retail shop scarcity alike increase accordingly. The invariable economic result of scarcity upon the prices of necessaries of life and their rise towards famine prices, naturally follows, and soon with discontent among the sufferers accordingly. This however can for a time be ignored, or viewed as mere popular "prejudice against improvement": generally, however, it is soothed down, with further promises of speedy rehousing in better conditions, and as soon as funds allow.

Meantime these Improvement funds increase, indeed sometimes beyond anticipations. For the large and deep sites along the new and spacious streets for business, and on the new avenues for dwellings, are attractive to all eyes; and thus arouse competition. They are hence inevitably taken up by a richer class than those dispossessed, and handsomely built accordingly, with encouragement towards more. This enhancement of site-values gives solvency and prosperity to the Improvement scheme, which gains the confidence of the public and of Government naturally also.

It is of the essence of capital to be keen to see and speedy to act on, any new line of approved gain. In this way the city's property market becomes active; and soon, in anticipation of further improvement, very active indeed. Speculation thus arises, increases, and even inflates: with resulting profit to the Improvement scheme accordingly; and at first with further public confidence accordingly: all the more because the members of its governing body are quite above speculating themselves. Old-fashioned householders, who would formerly no more have thought of selling their homes than their families, are thus attracted into the property-market by their growing confidence in the scheme and its management; merchants, formerly concentrated on their old legitimate business, are tempted in too: and values thus go on rising, even by leaps and bounds. But every speculative boom has its limit: the Banks, etc., apply this, by ceasing to advance on such property: with heavy losses to the last speculators, which however at first, seem but their own affair.

It has, however, been overlooked by all concerned—not excepting the Improvement Authority which started with the best intentions towards the people's housing and their smaller trade,—that its entire fabric of finance, and of increased property-values—the speculators' and the Trust's alike,—is based, to a very great extent, upon Scarcity rentals (and heightened prices also) to the people, which its demolitions could not but create and increase. Good intentions here have therefore proved not only useless, but worse; for, despite all hopes and promises, such Improvement authorities find themselves unable to rehouse, without loss or even disaster, more than a fraction (sometimes indeed but specimens) of the poorer population which they dispossessed, in hopes to improve. And even this measure of housing has too commonly to be mere warehousing; *i. e.*, in huge tenements, ("Chawls") with small single rooms, and at rents necessarily higher than of old. And—as "capital values must be maintained,"—this new environment, with its new forms of deterioration and insanitation replacing the old ones, is now too substantial and permanent ever to admit of the easy demolition of the preceding *kutcha* housing. The former large area of such one-storey buildings in towns had the advantage, in the peoples' interest, and so from their point of view, of keeping site-space at low value per acre, thus making such building easy and cheap. The "Improvement" methods derive their advantage, even their survival, from the opposite view-point and interest, that of the propertied and land speculating classes and their economists; by making site-space and working-class dwellings permanently and increasingly dear.

The popular dread of " Town-planning ", and distrust even of "Sanitation", which have thus been spread all over India (and are even plain here as elsewhere, when one goes through Patiala, plan in hand) are thus no mere surviving "prejudice", to be explained as conservatism, backwardness or ignorance ; as educated and governing classes, (Indian as well as British) are wont to think and say. On the contrary, this popular public opinion is only too well founded, in their bitter experience of too many would-be City-Improvement schemes hitherto—of dispossession, and increased over-crowding at heightened rents, with resultant rise of prices generally; in short of real suffering. That their inevitably resultant dissatisfaction, discontent, and distrust, are thus far too legitimate, my past eight years experience of very many of the leading cities of India, and of the results of their improvement schemes, (and in British India and Native States too much alike) has left me no option but to recognise. It thus compels me to offer the above broad analysis of the too prevalent situation, and as warning to Cities considering Improvement Schemes. For, with the best intentions in the world, it is only too easy to be led into such methods and conditions, and in practice very difficult to avoid them. For destruction is only too easy; reconstruction always difficult.

Of course these unfortunate tendencies and results are at length becoming more or less widely recognised, and endeavours are increasingly made to avoid them. Most conspicuous and most successful in this respect, so far as my knowledge goes, is the Improvement Trust of Lucknow, since this has grown with experience, of able Town Councillors, guided by an admirably devoted Deputy Commissioner, and a City Secretary no less so. For of its administration it is the principle that, though some dispossession, for demolitions, is of course inevitable, it must be accompanied by actual rehousing, and not postponed by mere hopes and promises of this. Its executive takes a legitimate pride in dealing individually with every case, and in finding a satisfactory new location before taking away the old one. No doubt it may thus, at times and at places, proceed more slowly; but such progress is sure: and it is moreover freed from the drag of popular dissatisfaction and reluctance; it is even increasingly winning general confidence and support instead. I am therefore fortunate in having been able to arrange, on the way through Lucknow to Patiala lately, not only for such information as may be desired, and for welcome to any State, Municipal, or other responsible visitors, from Patiala, who may desire to inspect its operations in Lucknow: and also, if desired, for affording a period of training under its admirable Executive Chief (Mr. W. Botting, formerly Municipal Secretary, and later City Executive Officer) for any officer of Patiala State or City who may be selected for the carrying out of improvements here.

B.—The Later Town-Planning Movement as Reconstructive and Constructive :—

CIVIC DESIGN.

This later movement of improvement and development has arisen more from the criticism of the previous school in particular, and of the utilitarian economics in general, than from following these; though it of course accepts and continues their elements of value. Its increasingly clear characteristics are two-fold: first, a larger view both of social and of individual life than as limited by its mechanical and monetary interests—especially as exaggerated, to the depression of others, by the recent phases of Western Civilisation, its " machine-economy " and " price-economy ". It is thus not contented with adding current sanitation to the preceding. It insists on the necessity of providing, more and more fully, for the completest possible improvement of the whole life-conditions of the community and its members—and these, as a leading American sociologist briefly puts them, are,—" health, wealth, sociability, beauty, knowledge and rightness ". This statement might be further developed, and thus clarified also in terms of social science, but may here suffice for the present.

The second character of the movement is that it increasingly bases this more comprehensive procedure upon a correspondingly full and varied " Survey ". This starts with the topographic survey—the town plan—with which the previous school was satisfied. But now it uses this as a basis of enquiry (and a means of record) which goes as fully as may be into all the above-named aspects of the community's life; in the past even, as well as in the present.

Place, Work and People, are thus scrutinised anew; and these separately, with the help of the geographer, the economist, and the anthropologist, (and historian too) who have long been in the field, each for his separate aspect. But these separate studies now here combine. Place admittedly determines, and limits, work—hence " place-work"—geographical and economic, (less accurately called "economic geography "). It also so far conditions people, as " place-folk ",—

as natives or as neighbours. But work also conditions the "work-place'— fields, in the country; workshop, factory, shop, office, etc., or in the town. Work too, in its division of labour into Occupations, produces as many different kinds of "work-folk," and these with their distinctive division again, as directive and executive,—masters and workmen, capitalist and labourers. But people also react on place—the "folk-place" is the home. And as these settle in their distinctive occupations, we have their "folk-work," which has been so great a factor in the establishment of caste, a world-phenomenon, though India affords its most crystallised examples.

These formerly separate studies, geographical, economic, and anthropological, are thus woven (and with their history) into one, as a beginning of the comprehensive science of Sociology; and with its applications in particular places and cases as Civics. This is but their simplest presentment, their introductory outline; yet enough here to indicate the needed comprehensiveness of every Social Survey.

Of such survey the Census is a good beginning; yet a early form, and too much stereotyped by bureaucratic tradition upon its first beginnings. Our Surveys, however, not only become increasingly historic as well as actual: they have to be psychological also. We are thus compelled to observe and consider the whole community, the whole region and city we are enquiring into, as far as may be in terms of their deeper and inner life and tradition. This inner life is at once emotional, intellectual, and imaginative, and in various forms, with their corresponding expressions in religion, education and art; and these have come through history to be very variously mingled in every city. How these three great interests again all interact (as into doctrines and philosophies for the learned, and into current ideas and habits for the people) cannot be ignored: since from these three main interests of the inward life—towards the good, the true, the beautiful, and their interactions—there have actually come the (past and present) essential traditions and characters of each main section of the Community,—in short its distinctive *worth* and culture, and its type accordingly, Hence our region and city under survey are not by any means so simply explained from the geographical, economic, and racial factors we started by recognising. The long separation between these two schools and methods of investigation —one insisting essentially on the material aspects and factors of every human society, and the other upon its spiritual factors and their outcomes—thus gives place to the more intensive study of both sets of factors; and these are found each to complement the other.

Only thus, with all these factors together, can we begin to understand the community in its various sections, and as a whole. We are now learning to understand its distinctive groups; in their customs and laws, their morals and manners; and thus to appreciate the various institutions which regulate these, which conduct its affairs, which guide its achievements; and which thus are ever modifying or restraining its changes, by their controlling influence over people, work, and place alike. It is now evident that the aspects and styles of a city's buildings, private as well as public, are thus determined by this whole preceding complex of factors ; and so are the various forms of the conduct of life.

To know and appreciate each and all the vital elements in the distinctive social groupings which make up this complex social situation of our city, and to strengthen these, by such fresh adaptations as may be, is already desired by all men of good will; but it is the task of Social Science to survey those more clearly. It thus prepares the way towards a fuller Co-operation of these vital elements, and as constructivo factors. Towards what end? The furtherance and enhancement of all that is best in the life of the community and its members,—now seen no longer as the mere struggling "Individuals" of past economic theory, but as "Socians" of an advancing Society, Citizens of no mean City.

Yet our survey still remains obviously incomplete, unless it be accompanied, and at all points, by a study of the Evils which infect and deteriorate the city, and thus injure or weaken its citizens' lives, unduly shortening life and lowering its efficiency. Sanitation is of course the beginning of this, and long recognised; yet we have now to take in all other aspects of social life to render even our simple sanitation successful. For the prevalent disease of modern times, and of India perhaps in particular, is not any one of the organic calamities, such as plague, malaria, etc. of recent sweeping visitations, of which Patiala's 821 ruins are so largely the lamentable monument. The essential evil lies in that lowering of nervous resistance and psychic vigour,—in short "neurasthenia"—which leaves people a too easy prey to these specific diseases. It is the now common urban prevalence of depressed physical tone, and of lessened mental and moral energy together. Of these evils the symptoms are only too manifest in the modern city. Hence its diminished economic energy and efficiency. Hence also its lessened material constructiveness, with lowering and almost cessation of art-interest, and of art-production, together. The modern city, despite its apparent bustle of business and buzz of machinery, is thus sick, sick at heart. With its emotional life fading to apathy, religion loses its vital energy, and servives mainly as routine. With depressed interest in life and its higher issues intellect is dulled, and education sinks to cram in early years, and oblivion afterwards. Imagination and the arts die down together; or are replaced by crude stimulants, dull comforts, or transient luxuries, in lower, middle and upper classes, respectively, or more or less together.

All this modern depression and deterioration of life in city, town and country, all these and kindred evils, from which every modern city is more or less suffering,—in India so manifestly, and thus here—have thus more and more searchingly to be surveyed. Their study is more urgent than ever since the War, and in view of these complicated states of social tension and unrest now more or less manifest in every country without exception; and with which not one has yet succeeded in successfully coping; since mere material restraint, however individually and externally necessary in given cases, does not cure either material or mental ills, still less both combined.

Here however we students of the Cities, with our survey and scrutiny of past and present social conditions of all kinds, and of these in their varied interaction, have long been quietly working out from such surveys some clues of interpretation, still commonly overlooked by specialists of all kinds. Thus some forty-five years ago the writer, then a student in Paris, still full of ruins from the War, and still more from the Commune of 1870-71, learned from the foremost and most experienced of its Mayors—at once also man of science and physician, historian, and philosopher, and statesman above all,—how the War and the Commune alike had not a little been excited through the economic tension, and thus the social unrest, brought about by the too sweeping reconstruction of Paris in the previous half generation; since this had resulted in giving all classes but the richest about half the accommodation for twice the rental. Similarly, for a good many years before 1914 we have been reading, upon the townplan of Berlin, such an accumulation of the factors of unrest, as in themselves sufficient to impel Prussia into war. Again, from almost lifelong knowledge of Ireland, both country and town, and particularly of its rival storm-centres, Dublin and Belfast, one has increasingly seen that the unrest of that country was not merely from the agrarian causes which have been at length diagnosed, and in parts successfully treated (as by agricultural co-operation especially). For, yet more profoundly, it arises in the condition of Irish towns and cities, in too many ways among the very worst in the world; but not yet adequately diagnosed, still less appreciably dealt with, whether by the State, the Municipalities, or by the various contending parties.

In short then, in the present position of social and civic science, it is becoming possible to reach a diagnosis of at least this great cause of social unrest, which is at any rate in substantial degree clearer and nearer the facts than have been the interpretations of any political parties, or any economic schools; whether Conservative, Liberal or Radical, Imperialist or Socialist, Capitalistic or Anarchistic. These parties moreover are still continuing to regroup themselves; on one side towards revolution, on the other side to repression: with the tragic condition of Russia as extreme sample of the resultant of such social conflict. Yet with our social and civic surveys before us, and despite their melancholy aspect, a corresponding hope appears: even a policy of reconstructive peace; in at any rate some substantial beginnings of Regional Renewal and of City Design. For in such city design all elements of the community, all its activities, can again find useful place and scope for career and service: and thus alike for age with its tradition, its experience, and its caution from the past; also for youth, with its restless energy, and its aspirations towards the future.

We claim, in fact, as students of social science, to be reaching conclusions as definite as to the nature and constitution of communities and cities, as to their normal development and functioning, as are those of physiological science for the individual. Furthermore, as the physiologist is becoming a pathologist, and next also a surgeon and physician, coping successfully with many diseases, though not yet with all, so the sociologist is beginning to understand some at least of the social evils; and even, as socian, and city designer, to combat them, and to abate them.

The progress and the applications of the simpler sciences, as of mechanics, of chemistry or physics, are no longer questioned either in peace or war. So too biological science and its applications begin to get their opportunity, as even in war, but still more in peace; in town in medicine and public health, in the country in agriculture, and by and by in both, as horticulture etc. It is now the turn of Social Sciences, and of their applications; and though these are latest to win a hearing, (for these can be of no service to conflict, whether of external war or internal disturbance) their town plannings and city designs are at any rate beginnings towards the vital re-establishment of social order, through the renewal of regional and civic progress.

A fresh cycle of Civic development, and of fuller individual life accordingly, may thus be entered upon.

On this view and policy of civic renewal, no city need wait, as all are more or less at present doing, for pacification over the great world, or for solution of all other economic difficulties and conflicts. On the contrary, such constructive work cannot begin too soon—"right here now", as the Americans say.

Yet with modest beginnings first, to which the following chapters are devoted, before proceeding to larger improvements, thus rendered far more simple, and less costly, than would at first appear.

CHAPTER V.

Mohindra College.

The Present Situation and its possibilities.

Here is a college of which we have not the like, taking buildings and grounds together in Bombay, Calcutta, or many other large cities; and which, when extended as proposed, will be on the great scale of the more spacious colleges of Oxford and Cambridge.

Educationally too, I understand it holds a good record, and so far as I can judge, it seems likely not only to maintain this, but advance on it. And,—without here going fully into the present University situation, in India and in Europe—it cannot be too clearly understood that a great transition is in progress, from the stereotyped Examination system based on that of London University before its recent educational developments. Of this change the recent Calcutta University Commission has given substantial evidence, as also the institution of a new University at Dacca. Yet still more impressive are the rise of the new Universities of Benares, Aligarh, etc., and the reorganisation, now in progress, of the Tata Research Institute at Bangalore. For research, in India, the Bose Institute of Calcutta is now world-famous; while European as well as Indian educators are also looking forward with keen interest to the University developments which Dr. Rabindra Nath Tagore is now adding to his already distinguished school.

Throughout Europe also, the old Universities are stirring; and not only those stimulated by victory, but also those aroused to new efforts, by defeat. New institutions of higher education are also arising, both on the small and experimental scale and on the great; and of these letter I may mention my own recent and current task, of designing for Jerusalem the largest and most comprehensively equipped of Universities hitherto; or further, of some collaboration in the scheme of the new "International University" already spaciously housed at Brussels, and under the patronage of the League of Nations.

Finally, and returning to India, I may cite, as an example of the changing attitude of Universities throughout the world, the recent formation of a committee in Bombay towards the collaboration of University and City. For in its initial circular is expressed the conception which has long been germinating in the "University Settlements" and "University Extension" systems of the West, but is now becoming understood and acted upon as a growing policy. Namely this, that beyond conserving the traditions of learning and science, or even advancing these by original research, the University has duties and possibilities of ever-extending usefulness to its City and Region. And further, that by utilizing these, it may best train and develop the powers of its students, and find useful outlets for them in many directions to the public advantage. The cultural advantages of the University are thus not merely further diffused throughout the City, but its material activities are advanced as well; and these in many ways, the scholars stimulating its printing, and the scientists its industries; while the university gains in turn, by associating the practical and experienced leading minds of the city in its deliberations and its management.

That Mohindra College is already ready for its part in this co-operation with the City, I have already had repeated experiences, and of different kinds. Thus in dealing with the public nuisance created by the very imperfect and old-fashioned management of the Distillery, the Professor of Chemistry has undertaken the necessary analyses. The planning of the Zoological and Botanic Gardens close by must bring together the professors of these subjects with the Government Departments of Forestry and Agriculture, with the experts in Silk Culture and in Chemical Industries also. Here we have in fact the main beginnings of an Agricultural College; and though there is as yet only teaching of the preliminary sciences of Medicine all minds in the college are more or less open to the interest of Public Health; hence vigilant and skilful aid in the reduction of Malaria, Plague and other evils may readily be recruited from the College.

That the present Model School has had to be temporarily lodged in the College is obviously a matter of mutual disadvantage. It is very desirable for the adequate space and working of each that a new location for the school be found outside, yet at convenient distance; and I plan for this accordingly (Chap. XVI.) As regards the development and location of Schools in gradually increasing numbers, and in ever-improving quality, the College can naturally render aid.

A good Professor of Education would be one of the most desirable of possible additions to the college staff; for instead of isolating young teachers in a separate Normal School, it is increasingly found far more satisfactory to train them in the larger and more educated atmosphere of the University.

Alike in discussing the further possibilities of the Co-operative movement in Patiala, and the difficult economic problems of its general improvement, I have found not only goodwill, but useful criticisms and suggestions from the economic learning of the College, as well as from the practical experience of State Officials, like the able and energetic Registrar of Co-operative Societies, and from members of the Municipal Council and others. In all these ways, and more, it is possible, and that increasingly here to bring College and City, thought and action, more fully together, and to mutual and general advantage.

Planning of College Extension.

By help of two excellent young surveyors kindly lent by the Chief Engineer, Sardar Rala Ram, I have been provided with a more accurate and larger-scale plan than heretofore; while Principal Sharma, in repeated walks together over the ground, has given me a clear statement of his requirements. The accompanying plan embodies these; and, I think I may now say, to his satisfaction.

Proceeding eastwards from the corner of the College Grounds nearest Moti Bagh, we pass the main College building, with no suggestion beyond that of slight (but speedy) repairs to the very topmost storey, (and mainly the balustrade) of its lofty and weather-beaten Towers. Just beyond this main building however, arises the question of the location of the needed new Science Laboratories. As to this, the situation indicated on plan will be most convenient in practice; since most conveniently reached from the existing College and Hostel buildings, etc., and least encroaching upon the existing Playing-fields on each side. This position will also be most effective architecturally, since giving the effect of a large and verdant Quadrangle, open towards the side of the public road, and thus at once contrasting with and combining the College front and side with the also handsomely arcaded south-west front of the Hostel, and its long plain south-east wall towards the road.

After the removal of the Potters' Village to its new locality (discussed latter), the needed New Hostel will naturally be erected upon its site, more or less as shown on plan. Between this new Hostel and the old one, space is left for the large Dining Hall, with Kitchens, etc., needed by this varied community of students.

The present Latrines will be easily moved to as convenient positions but less conspicuous; and here I trust, instead of the present methods of removal, the College may take the better method, at once of ancient China, and of modern and advancing agriculture, of immediate disposal under the all-sanitating earth, and for cultivated land thereafter.

Beyond this new Hostel, if not extended too near the existing brick Nala, there may be room for Servants' Houses, screened from Nala and space beyond by a row of trees and shrubs.

Exactly facing the Samania Gate may best be placed the Entrance Gate and main central Roadway of the College, which is then shown running practically straight past all the above-mentioned buildings.

Besides new Laboratory and Hostel accommodation, Professors' Houses are required: and the college will be greatly strengthened by its staff thus living in proximity and intellectual contact with their students, and with each other. These houses are certainly best provided (at once upon the available ground, and for the hours of isolation and quietness which the studious life requires, for its daily recuperation after teaching), in moderately detached situations, and with separate gardens as shown on plan, and not in one or more united blocks. In choosing these situations, advantage has been taken of the higher ground for the house, and of lower ground for garden: while the features of beauty, and of venerable associations, which are afforded by the various old temples beside or within the College grounds, will also be appreciated. Twenty-one Sites are thus indicated; and these can be built on gradually, as funds allow. When necessary, in the remoter future of college growth and staff increase, other sites can be found outside, yet within easy walk of the college.

The remaining ground will all be readily utilised for Gardens and for Playing-fields. The existing houses may mostly remaine.

Instruction in Medicine.

The College has already the means of preparation for the first Examination of the Faculty of Medicine *i. e.* Mathematics, Physics, Chemistry (even Organic), Botany and Zoology; and of its 80 Science Students a fair proportion are being prepared as the "Medical Group." When the (below discussed) Gardens are going, and when by and by the new block for Chemistry and Physics is complete, these facilities should be among the best anywhere. The adjacent Dispensary, which is shortly to be provided by the Municipality, will also be of stimulus to Medical Students.

Without going forward to the formation of a complete Medical School, which would be expensive, and for which Patiala and its Hospitals are hardly large enough, there is no reason to prevent the supply of conditions for the second year of Medical Studies also, when funds allow—those of Anatomy and Physiology. For these departments the spacious Hospital grounds may readily afford location.

Before this may arise a department of Bacteriology; of which there are already good beginnings. For not only is this subject of central importance to the practice of medicine and public health, and the continued advance of these, but also to agriculture—soil and crops, stock and milk products alike; and to industries,—sericulture or brewing and distilling, for example. Thus the present and long continued public nuisance from the distillery would long ago have vanished, and to its own great profit, were its present unscientific and wasteful operations brought under the criticism of the microscope, &c. as everywhere else since Pasteur's work has been understood and applied throughout the past generation.

Finally, though the Medical Student must leave Patiala after his first year preparation in Science, or by and by, even with above-mentioned developments, after two years; the facilities which such a large and well equipped Hospital affords to graduates assisting its permanent physicians, may be increasingly developed. With a head like Colonel Lane, not only of eminent record in Medicine and Public Health but actively interested in their progress, and ably seconded, as he also is, this fine Hospital will thus be increasingly important in the medical education of the Punjab, and with good effect upon its own progress.

The Female Hospital, with its distinguished Lady Physician, may similarly increasingly attract and utilise graduates from the Women's School of Medicine at Ludhiana, and with similar useful reaction on the City, and even on other towns of the State.

Instruction in Law.

Studies of Law are naturally carried on in a Metropolitan City: for though only more advanced students can (or should) take much active interest in the activities of the Law Courts, their atmosphere of actuality more or less penetrates the whole Law School, and abates the student's danger of too exclusive reliance upon book-work and lecture notes alone. This advantage of Patiala, with its High Court, gives it an advantage over most other small cities, and one which this College cannot but profit by.

Instruction in Technology. (See Chapter XXIV.)

CHAPTER VI.

Zoological and Botanic Gardens.

The large wild beasts, now too narrowly confined at the Baradari, and the birds, etc, in the garden of Colonel Mistri, make up an excellent beginning for a Zoological Garden, with a collection easily and inexpensively, if gradually, increased. For locating this, I have first examined the large triangle of cultivated land lying between three wide avenues immediately to the west of the College; but this has the threefold disadvantage of being level and cultivated, and thus of being expensive accordingly. The deer-tribe may no doubt be shown to advantage upon level ground, laid out as a park; but the great wild beasts show far better in correspondingly wild situations and the more irregular and even jungly-looking, the better and more effectively. Thus after the experience of designing the Scottish Zoölogical Park at Edinburgh some years ago, in which the advantages of a varied site, level, rocky, and hilly by turns, have been utilised to afford characteristic habitats for different animals, so that their photographs appear as if taken in their natural surroundings, I have no hesitation in selecting the at present unpleasing area, a dry waste in great part, S. W. of the College, and ranging from Jacob's Outfall down to the City-Drain, and thence to the red hills of Brick-makers' waste beyond. Much of this land is already State property, and yielding (and thus costing) nothing; and the necessary intervening purchases of patches of irrigated and well cultivated land between, have, as the plan shows, been kept small.

Unpromising though this site looks, I have no hesitation in staking my credit—as through life a planner of gardens, and these both botanical and zoological, and with beauty of effect constantly in view—upon the affirmations (1) that this, of all possible sites in or around Patiala, is the most desirable on all these grounds, and (2) that here also the best effects can be produced with least expense—expense, in fact, unprecedentedly small for any such undertakings.

Alike for variety and interest of effects, and for economy of management and labour of upkeep, I here plan botanical and zoological collections together, yet with all due distinctness. The present creditable beginning of a Botanic Garden in a corner of the College lawn would naturally be transferred to this, with its Professor's and its mali's activities also.

A first example, of how difficulties of ground are also opportunities, is afforded by the high and dry ridge and slope from the neglected mounds excavated from Jacob's Outfall, down to the road leading to the old Forest Garden, now occupied by the Champion wrestler. Below the rough hedge by this roadside the cultivated land begins, and with good water supply, while at lowest runs the City drain, (happily well flushed and with sufficient current to be unobjectionable.)

Poor though may be the first impression of this area, one may must ask, where else among the Botanic Gardens of the world could one find a better site than these 200 yards of slope ?—since ranging, as it does, from ground with only Kikar (Babul) trees, to ordinary irrigated ground; and below this to ground easily enriched by manurial waters from the drain when need be. For here, and first of all, we can have the characteristic desertic vegetation of India, not only the Kikar (Acacia Arabica) and the gorgeous Dhak (Butea frondosa), but many of their allies, also of economic interest as well as beauty. Here too the Agaves and Aloes, with their manifold interest, not only to gardener and botanist, but to economist and physician. Here too, the hardier Eucalyptus species and other Australians, the cactus, and prickly pears, and many more; in short, the drought-resisting plants of the "Rock Gardens" of great collections, though here we need not go to expense for rocks almost at all. Lower down, below the hedge, there will flourish the more ordinary plants of cultivated and moistened soil; while at bottom there is scope for experimental richer cultures. In short these 200 yards will now range in vegetation from the dry lands of the Punjab and Rajputana to the wet delta of Bengal; indeed in flora, as the collection, grows, from the Arabian and the Australian desert-borders to "the Flowery Land", as China rightly calls herself. And for general view-point, especially of the lower garden, the little plateau with the fine Banyan tree near the Forest Garden entrance affords its shade. And this big tree may easily have its roots guided so as to form before long a concentric range of columns—a Garden Hall.

Everything is thus utilised, and inexpensively, except the rough roadside hedge. But this is the best opportunity of all: now for the zoologist, with his birds. For instead of the costly and narrow caging of the old Zoological Gardens, in which the birds sat imprisoned and forlorn, we have now simply to drive in a row of stout posts on each side of the hedge, and close it in on each side and above with wire-netting. Partitions of course are supplied at intervals, to keep each group of birds distinct, and safe, from its neighbours. But this inexpensive mode of construction is kept narrow enough to show the birds within only a few feet of the eye. It admits of length enough between each partition to give them a good flight along the length of their cage, so that they can practically live as if they were not caged at all. And that the visitor has now to look for them, in their hedge-clusters, and does not see them all at the first glance, gives him much of their interest and charm in nature, and something too, of the interest of seeking them there. Nesting too goes on in these conditions, and can be easily helped when necessary.

Of course the hedge is easily kept down by annual or more frequent cutting and pruning: but this not of course in any too regular way, but leaving plant-nature also as free and varied as may be.

But the spectator's Walk on either side of this hedge-long Flight Aviary (and of course with crossings at intervals between), is sunny and hot, and so needs shade. But for this again no expensive construction is required; merely a second row of posts on each side of those bearing the wire-netting of the Aviary, with higher ones binding them above, and then cross-bars or longwise bamboos between, and thus above the walk. We have thus an inexpensive "Pergola", one of the most splendid resources of gardening. It is used of course in gardens everywhere, and remains of two or more pergolas are in the Baradari, where some fine climbers are also growing well—bright purple Bougainvillea, the huge white-flowered Elephant-creeper (Bauhinia sp.) and various orange Bignonias, with of course occasional herbaceous creepers also, Convolvulus of two or three kinds, pink and white Antigonon and

Quisqualis, changing from white to red. But these few common forms are but a suggestion of the varied beauties and wonders of the climbing and twining flora of India, enriched too as this has been by introduction from all the tropical and warm temperate lands of the New World as well as of the Old. Yet nowhere in India, so far as I can learn, has any extensive collection been made; for though the expense of seed or cuttings is but trifling, and the labour of attention also peculiarly slight, sufficient space is not easily obtained, as fortunately here. For the main attention, of pruning this long range of climbers so as not to choke each other, or too darkly shade the birds, a single mali, with step-ladder and shears, may suffice.

We now come to the Public Road which passes from the College Road towards the main Canal. Looking across this from the end of the Pergola, the near view centres on a fine old square Tomb, with low dome. Before coming to this is a large Brick-makers' pit, long disused, and with its irregular, and partly over-grown edge, yielding an excellent picture, since containing water during great part of the year. This can be easily deepened a foot or two more, yielding earth to enlarge its little island. Fresh water too can be easily brought in from the neighbouring irrigation channel. Thus we have here, all but ready made, a perfect Pool for the Water Birds, who can shelter and nest in the adjacent hedge while the little Island, after a suitable tree has been planted for a few years, will supply at once a safe prison, yet of climbing freedom, for such monkeys as will not cross water. A separate pool for water-loving birds needing isolation like the Pelicans, can easily be excavated in the low ground below the Tomb (and also when need arises, small pools can be made where water stands beside the brickwork piers on the other side of the public road). But these will only be needed in future years, and as the collection grows.

The small vegetable garden on the high ground beside the Tomb, is, I understand, outside the State property, but will not cost much in money compensation, or land exchange, as may be arranged It will make an excellent Flower Garden, and also afford shaded seats for views into the bird pool, and over the lower ground eastward. Some portion of this low ground should also be acquired, to afford paddocks for deer, etc. with a path or rustic bridge leading across the Drain and to the hills of brick-rubbish. For among these are the places for the Dens of the great wild beasts, lions, tigers, and panthers, bears, etc: all easily arranged, as at Edinburgh, etc., so as to be really safely confined against escape, yet shown against a rocky background built up against the hill side; while prevented from leaping at the spectator by a water pool between.

In such ways then, beasts and birds are readily provided for; while peacocks, pigeons, etc. can easily be encouraged in freedom. As minor accessories to be added by degrees as funds allow, may be mentioned a Snake and Reptile-House. Also with advantage a small Insect House, primarily for increasing public interest in silk-culture, but also instructive and beautiful in rearing other insects—as at times for liberating swarms of butterflies which will brighten the flower gardens around and also teach student, schoolboy and public how flowers are fertilised.

Finally at end of the little Insect-house, there may be easily kept going by the professor of zoology, or any of his students, a demonstration of the life-history of the Mosquitos, and particularly of the small fishes which eat them up in the larval state. And with this again what could be more useful, more inexpensive, more profitable, to the health of the whole city and community, than two small hatching and rearing pools for these inestimably useful fishes, and for distributing them at the outset of the fever season, to all suspected tanks and pools? Here for instance is educative training for Boy Scouts, indeed for any school-boys not yet so fully trained.

The advantage of the Zoological and Botanic Garden to the College will not be overlooked; yet as an old investigator and teacher in both subjects I may add assurance that such rare proximity should make the College in these respects one of the most fortunate, in India or elsewhere.

From the European point of view the most imposing figures of a Zoological Garden, and these equalling, if not surpassing in popular interest, the great carnivores themselves, are the elephants, of which in Europe we see so few. No European collection can compare with Patiala, with its dozen or thereby; and though the Indian eye is accustomed to them from infancy it also realises their impressiveness in grouping, and above all their endlessly amusing aspect and behaviour when taking their bath. Here then, greatly daring, let me plead for this great collection to be added to the Zoo. They will be a little nearer both to Moti Bagh and even to the Qila; *i. e.* for processional use when required, and also not much further from any other work some of them occasionally have to do; while as we shall see later, good town-planning use can be made of their present area. I therefore suggest on plan for their location the next piece of higher ground further east from that for wild beasts. This has no difficulty of access, the Nala being crossed by substantial girder-bridges.

In this new location it is also easy to display the elephants, like the other animals, with much of their picturesqueness in nature, by judicious planting and grouping of trees aud bamboos, to serve as their background, yet out of reach of destruction by them; as also to provide bathing pools in the low ground below their plateau.

Finally may we not similarly provide for the State Camels? and even for the Oxen as well? For some, at least, if not all?

Completion of Zoological and Botanical Garden Scheme as Park.

Beyond this area no further ground positively needs to be acquired; yet beyond the first three brick-hills planned for the Lions' Dens, etc, we soon come to three more, also picturesque in colour and well tufted with Kikar trees. So, as these hills are unproductive, and as no other hills are obtainable in Patiala, may we not also add them to our park? The views of the city from their tops reward their visitors; and for good paths along their length, and between, these need but a little of the simplest spadework. So as the ground narrows here—between the canal avenue and the (good, but as yet treeless) road some way south of the Samadhan, until they meet midway between the fine Serai Maijiki and the Ghalori Gate—we have thus about a mile of Park and Parkways, from our start between College and Palace and our ending here; and all at an expense of which, as promised at the outset, the estimates will work out but small. It may safely be said, even surprisingly small, in comparison especially with the ordinary cost of such Parks and Gardens elsewhere. Yet since the success of Parks and Gardens may be broadly judged by the variety of interesting features and walks they contain, and correspondingly by that of the pictures and photographs they will yield, it will be seen that the present scheme is more varied than most. The common advantage and interest of City and College has been kept in view from the outset; and also the growing magnificence of the Moti Bagh Gardens which may be expected from so eminent a gardener as Mr. Burrows will gain an outdoor extension of drives and walks, of wilder contrast and of different interest also, from all this plant and animal variety, of nature and its utilisation.

Possible Agricultural Developments.

Again, if and when the College can add to its staff a Professor of Agriculture (for whose teaching the preliminary Sciences are mostly already there) the acquirement of some of the ground not at present asked for will still further develop the utilities of the present scheme, add yet far from injure its amenities in any way. In the interests not only of the College or of the City-Region, but of the whole productivity and prosperity of the State, I plead strongly for this modest additional outlay, the more since this will carry with it the better and more effective utilisation of all the existing departments of Science. For the Department of Agriculture is all but entirely here already.

AGRICULTURAL EXAMPLE:

Utilisation of Patiala Drain for Irrigation Meadow.

So, as a planner has to be man-of-all-work, let me for the moment take this proposed professor's place, and give an instance of the kind of service he should render. As agriculturist, I set my ambitions towards better crops, and hence desire not only irrigation, but good manure, and plenty of it. Hence this big Patiala Drain, in which both these possibilities are running to waste, peculiarly excites my attention, and even cupidity! I therefore follow it down, past its covered section through the Moti Bagh quarter, to its outlet in the forest below—and am surprised to find this worse and more objectionable than I could have expected! First, owing to a long-standing pool of back-water, fermenting and smelling as the drain did not do above,

Then below this an irregular and widening stream-bed, deep in refuse and ill-smelling mud—unpleasant in itself and spoiling the beauty and freshness of the forest. There too was the ugliest accident: a big bullock-cart, with three strong oxen, heavy-laden with sacks of flour, fully and firmly stuck midway across the stream in this loathsome mud, while four men, shoving with might and main to help the oxen, were powerless to move either forward or back; and all this with darkness coming on.

To remedy all these evils, and convert this spoiled area into fertility and even beauty, the expense is slight. Merely the labour of closing off the backwater, and levelling on each side of the stream-bed, so as to afford a long strip of irrigated land. This may here, with least disturbance to the forest, and probably the best and most productive return also, be laid down in grass for fodder, which will yield many and excellent cuttings. For this simple treatment there are many examples, notably the one oftenest cited, even in Indian books on Sanitation, that of the Edinburgh Sewage Irrigation-meadows, which though of the poorest sandy soil originally, have gone on, for many years yielding record crops, and with no offence to their neighbourhood. Here in Patiala, where fodder is certainly none too abundant, this will be found still more profitable, while the forest will recover its pleasantness as well. Nor can I offer a plainer example of how planning, with very moderate outlay, can yield a good return.

I might give similar instances, of how the zoologist and the botanist and bacteriologist may all co-operate; and with technical efficiency and economic result accordingly, where they are not already themselves discussing and devising these. Enough however, if an example like the above may serve to show how a College Agricultural Department can justify its Farm. And this indeed in more ways than by direct return, since suggestive to other farming and gardening, as well as educational to its students; and this in practical ways as well as in Science.

Patiala Pasturage and its Improvement.

There has above been pointed out the easy transformation of the nuisance-outlet stream of the main drain of Patiala, into a long irrigation meadow, yielding what would be unprecedented grass crops, and of the best quality, and suitable alike for use as fresh fodder, for drying as hay, or for preservation in the undried state as ensilage: so now this next naturally raises the question how far the existing pastures outside Patiala can also be improved: for that this is necessary and desirable. the too commonly poor condition of the cattle, and the small yield and high price of milk, are obvious proofs.

Why not also possible ? The large pastures east of the Canal are of too broken levels, largely from old brick-makers' pits etc. Why not a gradual levelling, (and again why not this with military leadership and aid ?) so as to admit of such irrigation, section by section, as may be. Even though partial and occasional, it would be of value, in appreciable percentage, the more since such levelling gives something of tillage. But these meadows are poor, the manure of the cattle being too much taken away for fuel, so that exhaustion of the soil goes on. A top-dressing, however, is possible, by carting out and scattering upon the areas levelled, and best before irrigation, or before the rains, some of the ample rubbish of the town's Kholas and other highly manurial matter. Thus the donkeys' field near the Corn-market would yield several feet for over its area; while the various cleansing depots of the town should also contribute their surface-layers.

The above treatment is surely worth a trial on a convenient unit of the pasture-area, which has at most to be temporarily fenced in by a wire, until the new growth is sufficiently advanced to admit of grazing on again.

Vegetables and Fruit in Patiala.

I am credibly informed that these are dear; and I learn this without surprise. Nor are these scarcity prices compensated for by any high quality in the products: on the contrary, the average is obviously mediocre, not to say generally poor, with exception perhaps for cauliflower and cabbage. Nor can anything better, if indeed so much, be said for the various kinds of fruit to be seen in shops and market.

No doubt good exceptions to these criticisms can be shown ; yet not until these exceptions have become the average, will Patiala market gardens be on the level of better ones, as of Lucknow etc.; and it has next to be remembered that these also are seldom up to what they might be. Each place no doubt has its specialities : thus Bombay mangoes, Nagpur oranges, Gwalior guavas, etc., have favourable conditions and traditional skill behind them. Still nothing but the too prevalent and too persistent inattention to good stocks and good varieties, to the skilled tending of these, and to the due enrichment of the soil also, can explain this too general mediocrity, here alleged of the mass of Patiala garden produce.

All this of course, is not for fault-finding's sake, but for encouragement and hope : for since horticulture survives, as it is, much may it improve and profit, when stock and seed, soil and its manure-supply are better attended to. Here may be a notable use for the small but varied Botanical Garden above ; for as it develops, it may readily afford a variety of convincing demonstrations to the gardeners of Patiala of what can be done with the aforesaid care of variety and seed, of soil and manure ; and with avoidance of over-watering as well as of under-supply. Very particularly, with that leadership at once in science and in skill, for which a Botanic Garden stands, it should help in that relation between the cleansing of the city and the enrichment of the surrounding horticulture, tillage and pasturage which has been above pointed out as admitting and needing imovement.

More and Better Vegetables and Fruit for Patiala.

Nothing would at once improve the quantity and quality of the Vegetable and Fruit supply of Patiala, as well as also lower prices to the consumer, though making the producer also more prosperous than before, than the better organisation of the cleansing of the city in direct relation with the development and improvement of its market gardens. Here is in fact one of those many cases in which the collaboration of different lines of work may be made fruitful to all. The Sanitary and Cleansing Department of the city, the Agricultural Department, and the Registrar of Co-operative Societies—in due consultation with their staffs, and with the cultivators—might readily here co-operate more fully than at present, and to the advantage of all concerned: and thus the entire community in the long run. The traditional prejudices, which at present keep India behind Japan and China in this matter of gardening, are already giving way: and need not long delay improvement.

CHAPTER VII.

Developments Kindred to Preceding.

Fuel and Timber.

In the current and increasing rise of prices of the necessities of life from which India is so severely suffering, that of Fuel is prominent. More slowly too than for any other commodity, can remedy be found for this; indeed it goes from bad to worse, since proprietors of forests are cutting too much without re-planting. How building and even repairing are hindered by the high cost of timber, is again a great and growing difficulty.

In the countries of Northern Europe—all more advanced in this respect than the comparatively forestless British Isles—replanting by forest proprietors is enforced; and it is most desirable to introduce such regulations here, since at once in the public interest and in that of the estates concerned.

In the United States, which have been too long cutting down their forests without replacement, the resulting disasters to the country, and the heightened prices to the town, have at length led to the policy of "Conservation of Natural Resources", vigorously established under President Roosevelt. But public opinion had been prepared for this during the previous generation through the institution of that most admirably useful of School holidays—"Arbor Day". Many millions of trees have thus been planted in American Cities and towns, suburbs and villages, and the parents and public are now educated in the matter accordingly. The French Government also introduced this holiday some years ago, and it has many advocates in Britain. In India also, indeed in Patiala, I have found an able and energetic plea for its adoption; which I can have no hesitation in recommending to the consideration of the Education Department. The Boy Scouts—now also so successfully initiated in India by that foremost of all British Educationists, General Sir R. Baden-Powell, are naturally taking to this work, and are available for more than a single school holiday.

In this connection too, since the main labour required is that of digging the holes, cannot substantial aid be given by the military ?

The War has proved the literally vital necessity of trench-digging, and this with the utmost rapidity, needing not only strength but skill. But this heavy work cannot be made congenial in peace time, when trench-making has only to be filled up again: whereas here is a useful outlet for it, in which the labour thus becomes of interest, and can be speedily and effectively done accordingly, and even with that element of rivalry which is so stimulating to vigorous youths and men. The Boy-Scouts will thus get a standard to work up to. Much may thus be done for the city and its neighbourhood.

Larger Scale Forestry; and Funds for it.

The above, it will be truly said, may be all very well for cities and towns, even villages with their spare labour at some periods, and their after all moderate requirements in the matter of shade and fruit trees; but it does not meet—nor even more than touch—the fringe of the larger needs; of Fuel and of Timber.

The Forest service in all countries—than which no State Departments can be more efficient—is able and willing to meet these requirements as soon as may be; but it lacks the necessary funds. These were never so needed as at present—for as a wise American statesman has lately pointed out, even the War-debts can best be met by Governments through a vigorous policy of afforestation. Yet every State-exchequer is but a taxation-bank, and hard-pressed enough to meet immediate claims; while financiers have to keep their money fluid, and cannot invest for forest returns, which however promising, are too slow for them. Private individuals, young and old alike, have also their obvious reasons for holding back from such investment. The result is that the forester is pleading almost in vain. No funds, in any sufficient quantity, seem available for him from any quarter.

Yet there remains one source, from which, with due organisation, he can increasingly obtain the enlarging annual amounts he so urgently requires. For there remains one source of annual ready money still untapped—the most regular, and not least substantial, of all forms of saving, that devoted to Life Insurance, with its annual premiums, so regularly paid, on pain of forfeiture of the policy itself.

Why not then, in and for the benefit of every State, its Foresting Insurance Company? The conventional investments of premium income by the ordinary Insurance Companies, are, and have to be, in the most substantial securities, of land mortgages, railway debentures, etc; and thus they yield only a very moderate rate of interest. But here, in forestry, is substantial security also; with yield of interest indeed small, (say zero) in the first three or four years, but thereafter a steadily rising rate, and with prospect of substantial increase as soon as felling fully begins, with fuel trees especially. After ten years then, the Forest Insurance Company would fully be getting into its stride of progress; and thereafter it should be able to give its policies a bonus, rivalling, even before long surpassing, that possible to Insurance Companies of the customary type. It would moreover save most of what these companies now spend in rivalries of advertisement; and its management would be also less costly, since mainly performed by the existing Forest Department maintained by Government, and already under supervision; with only the necessary addition of actuarial and clerical assistance. It would moreover be on the mutual basis, without profit to shareholders for establishing it.

Safety can be given by dividing premium investments between the various forests; and if necessary by giving the general guarantee of the existing State forests also. Loans may be advanced, for planting, to landed proprietors and on the usual security; yet with the advantage, that this is spent (as with an Agricultural Bank) on definite improvement of the security, instead of merely on ordinary mortgage independent of this,—a notable advantage for the Forest Insurance Companies.

The difficulty of this scheme is of course at once obvious :—What of the claims which inevitably come in from premature deaths?—and before the new Forest Insurance Company is beginning to get in a return from its young forests enough to meet them? This difficulty can however be easily met, and in either of two ways, or both together; *viz.*,—(1) by reinsurance in existing companies for these premature calls, of which the normal and extremes are percentages with which Insurance Tables have long been clearly supplied. Also (2) if need be, this reinsurance can be more cheaply met by the ordinary, (and normally increasing) yield of the present State Forests, which can recover such advances as the new Forest grows up to meet them.

In short, then, it is submitted that such a scheme as outlined can be worked up in detail for Patiala State by a committee essentially of the Forestry experts, with advice from a competent Insurance Actuary; and with Banker and Business men to aid their deliberations. Their scheme would then be scrutinised by the Government; and at length, when finally adjusted in every particular, it would be ready for its appeal to the public. That at first only a moderate proportion of new insurers would respond is not altogether a disadvantage. These would be of more active mind, accessible to ideas like this, of combining their own family's advantage with that of the public: and such men tend to live longer than average, and hence might thus not inappreciably lower the percentage of premature claims; though this would of course still be fully provided for.

In short, then, our current and increasing timber and fuel difficulties may be before long effectively grappled with, and this with useful re[illegible] upon the promotion of thrift, and the advance of Insurance methods towards productive use and public advantage in their most substantial forms.

I therefore venture respectfully to submit that this proposal be considered by representatives of Forestry, Insurance, Banking, etc., with instructions to report to the Durbar upon its practicability, now or later.

Silk Industry for Patiala.

With regard to this industry—so important if it can be fully set agoing, and so valuable also in its social reactions upon the community—a few suggestions may be permitted—of course without prejudice to the admirable and devoted labours of Sirdar Vazir Chand, but entirely in hopes of assisting these. Here, as elsewhere in India, the main endeavour has been primarily to interest the rural villages; but here in the Punjab, more than elsewhere, the silk-worm rearing comes at a busy time for the peasant. Is it not therefore necessary to reach him also indirectly? For this the Schools offer a convenient agency; and a reference to Indian School magazines will give many examples of its success in interesting girls and boys alike. Moreover every State tends to follow the example of its Capital; so if the leading schools of Patiala set the example, provincial schools will readily follow it.

So let us plant Mulberry trees in the borders of the School compounds, and as a beginning of the School Garden, which is so important a factor in educational life as it recovers from that exaggeration of book-work alone, which has been so characteristic of the instruction of the past. And even if not soon and actively used for silk-rearing, the tree is beautiful and fruitful (and fodder-yielding too); so deserves encouragement on all these grounds as well. It is also here to be noted that this policy, of starting silk-growing largely through the children, has not to wait till they grow up: for parents are thus educated though their sympathy with their childrens' interests and pursuits; and it is also a great gain to have the teacher active in this matter, from which he too can derive matter for many valuable lessons.*

Again why should not silk growing be encouraged in the towns? and here in Patiala? It is indeed especially a woman's industry; and on the lines of her feeding and life-tending interests and instincts. Given then a Silk Department, with an adequate Mulberry plantation at convenient distance outside the town, (and thus able to provide dust-free leaves, a matter of importance), it could readily supply not only good "seed" (eggs) as is usually done—but fresh leaves also—conveniently in tins which will keep a two days' supply fresh, and thus lessen labour of delivery. It can then take over the cocoons (unkilled if need be, to spare Hindu reluctance towards the taking of life) and pay for its services by retaining a proportion of the resultant silk. The winding is again a woman's industry, which can be prosecuted in the home; as other silk industries are already in Patiala.

The man delivering the Mulberry leaves can also keep an eye on the rearing, and so prevent the mistakes of which the fatal results so readily discourage beginners. Clean mats and trays can also be brought by him at the outset of the season, and paid for in cocoons at the close.

---

* I am told that there is an objection to silk-worm rearing as of bad odour. But this is merely an index of bad tending, and easily corrected by ordinary care. This industry in fact peculiarly needs clean surroundings for its success, and thus tends to react favourably upon the home which practises it.

Passing now to the uses of silk, a little encouragement from the ladies of Patiala would soon spread through the city. And though in India embroiderers are so often men, there is no reason to prevent women, as in other countries, here taking an active share, and working out specialities of their own. Turkish, Chinese and Japanese embroideries all find ready markets in Europe and America, and so will Indian, as they become available. Here again the Girls' Schools could take a fertile initiative.

Fish for Patiala.

Despite the fact that many do not eat fish, and that the fish in the great Tank beside the Daviji Temple are protected by its sanctity, it may safely be said that there is here more of natural demand than of actual supply, and with high prices of course accordingly. For hereabouts there seems to be little or no fishing to speak of.

A similar backwardness as to inland fish culture has prevailed in Britain since the Reformation; hence the first man of active initiative in this matter is within my own memory; and thus is explained that indifference to pisciculture which has been prevalent among my countrymen in India, however otherwise progressive.

Even in Bengal, the land of fish-eating par excellence, it is news to most Bengalis as practically to all others, be they Indian or British, that in that rich delta, so well watered by its rivers and so productively cultivated also, any ordinary untidy and unwholesome-looking tank may be yielding a return three or four times greater than that of the well tilled land beside it. Still more is it surprising, yet I believe incontestably proved, that given the same intelligent care as that of the peasant for his soil, the tank can yield seven times better.

Now if this be so, why should not every Department of Agriculture start an initiative towards fisheries? The Madras Government has lately found the needed man and already with admirable results. It is thus only a question of the time needed for communication of ideas for other Governments to follow suit. Why not here?

In dry regions of old in India, as also so notably in Ceylon, the levels of the land were taken with fully adequate (and even remarkable) surveying skill; and dams were erected, of which the engineering, and the irrigational efficiency, have also been justified through ages. Beyond local surface irrigation, these great tanks rendered the immense geographic service of keeping up the water-level in the soil; whereas the steady fall of this (increasing too, as it goes on doing, even within living and recent experience) has been a great factor in the impoverishment of Indian agriculture.

Now that the importance of such matters is being increasingly realised, and by geologists, foresters, agriculturists and engineers alike, it is safe to predict that this matter of Tank-making will soon be increasingly pressed upon Indian Governments, as so notably of late years in Ceylon. Of course when reservoirs can be on high enough level to yield electric power, there is now no fear of their speedy construction; and even from private capital; but the difficulty is thereby only increased for collecting areas little above their plain. Without asking for any new engineering of importance, two points may here be asked (1) that wherever there survives a transverse bund, even broken, it may be considered for repairs? These repairs may sometimes be made by adjacent agricultural villages, in their own interest.(It may even be asked whether in a district with longitudinal bunds, like those east of Patiala, some of the water they provisionally enclose may not at convenient points be utilised? Depending of course on levels above and below the city, and with all care for its protection as at present). The second question is this—cannot this tank-making process be accelerated by the prospect of return from Fish-culture?—and especially if this prove more profitable than agriculture?

Pending any tank-making however, for which public (and even official) opinion in India is as yet hardly ready, I plead for the practical test, meantime, of fish-culture in such tanks, lakes, ponds (and even permanently full portions of canals, or ends held up) as may be available. The process is inexpensive: simply to stock them with the right fishes, already known in each province, and then see how they grow. For that is with a tropical rapidity of which higher animals give no idea.

Futhermore, had I a tank in Bengal, I would expect soon to be getting even better results than even sevenfold the land beside, after a few experiments in feeding the fish, and this by the almost costless method recently introduced in Scottish lochs and lakelets, and found successful beyond anticipation; that of simply tossing into the water here and there, and from time to time, a bundle of weeds, tied by a string and sunk with stone or half brick inside. Their slow, gentle decomposition does not defile the water; for its germs, etc., are eaten up by larger microscopic creatures, these by small crustaceans, these by small fish, and these again by the bigger ones. The agriculturist has always seen to feeding his stock; but the fisherman is now finding out that it pays him to do the same.

Fish and Malaria.

Though at the time of R. B. Ganga Ram's thoroughgoing abolition of the Tobahs of Patiala, there seemed no alternative to the costly filling up of Malaria-producing tanks, save the objectionable one of keeping their surface constantly oiled, we now know that it is only necessary to keep tanks clean, with tidy banks and free from weeds, by a little regular care, and see to them being stocked with fishes, especially of the right mosquito-larva eating sorts. All easy matters, requiring at most only the ordinary routine care of a decent Mali, once he has grasped his job. Thus it is, that even without much care, the fine big Mall Tank of Patiala does not yield so many mosquitos as will a single puddle by the wayside, much less the neglected drain from a single home. Any small tank, however, without fish, as apparently at several temples in or outside Patiala, must be a source of Malaria demons, very discreditable to its sacred character; yet easily got rid of by roughly cleansing and then stocking, and without oiling, still less filling. Is it not a pity, and even a shame, that Temples, which not so long ago were setting the standards of cleanliness as well as of moral and spiritual life to their neighbourhoods, should thus now be standing as centres for dirt, disease and death; and diffusing these around?

Happily the present cleansing of the great Amritsar Temple Tank is an example of that returning union of cleanliness and godliness on which all religions were wont to agree; so in this the older faiths cannot much longer fail to follow.

Further Developments of Agricultural and Technical Industries. See Chapter XXIV.

Industrial Development and Economic Value of Health.

In spite of the increasing interest throughout India in its economic development, its discussion has as yet two defects. First, as mainly turned towards urban and mechanical industries, with altogether in sufficient attention to the improvement of agriculture, as incomparably the most important of all—a matter on which it suffices here to refer to the new book of Mr. H. Calvert; *Wealth and Welfare in the Punjab* (Lahore, Civil and Military Gazette Press, 1922, Rs. 6). For in this the case for Rural Development is not only admirably stated; but also that for Rural Economics, as contrasted with the far too strictly urban and market economics, at present predominant alike in Cities and, Governments, Legislatures, etc., as in the Colleges and Universities and those in India as well as in Europe.

Second, in discussing Indian economic development, far too little recognition is yet given to the fact that the average expectation of life throughout India is still as low as that of England in its early industrial age a century ago: and it is hence too much overlooked that the greater wealth and productivity of the West is essentially associated with the fact that its workers have now, broadly speaking, nearly twenty years of longer prime, available for productivity. This matter is discussed more fully in my Report to the Durbar of Indore, and hence need not be again enlarged on here; suffice it to press the point that whatever measures of sanitation, housing, better food supply, etc., can be taken in this, or any other Indian city, they should not be looked upon as improductive disbursement: but on the contrary be realised as the most fertile and lucrative form of investment possible to any community—that of the extension of its effective and productive life. Nor is this simply a matter of years of life: but also of their quality: every day's sickness is a loss to the community: hence the reduction of malaria is inestimably profitable, beyond its mere reduction of death-rate.

CHAPTER VIII.

Cleansing, Whitewashing, &c: Aspects of Patiala.

Cleansing of Patiala.

After a prolonged study of the town which has not left a single lane unvisited, it would be most inappreciative not to leave on record the resulting, and favourable, impression, of the really high (in fact unusually thorough and high) standard of cleansing which the Municipality maintains throughout its streets and lanes, its drains also, both great and small.

There remain, however, several serious drawbacks, (1) the standing temptations to the sweepers, afforded by the 821 Kholas, for lightening their burdens; (2) the often very unpleasant, and always very unwholesome, Depots of daily accumulations, which so obviously, and often so deplorably, deteriorate their neighbourhood. A single example of this may suffice, the spoiling of the fine wide open space on Nala Kanerian Street; but all the other Depots are more or less open to the same criticism.

I am informed that this state of things is fixed by the arrangement with contractors: but after all, public health is not a matter for contracts: contracts are for the public's health. Again, (3) the carts employed are wholly unsuitable, with their open sides, through which the contents are obviously spilling out, upon the street, and into the air. Proper removal carts, with solid sides, and with lids folding in from each side, are alone adequate for this work; and these are in use in most cities. I am informed indeed that the Municipality formerly possessed such carts, but that they have worn out. I can only plead that they renew them: no sanitary outlay can be more legitimate or desirable. (4) The sweepers also are too much using mere baskets, without adequate provision of barrows: if so, this too requires increase.

All no doubt expensive; yet there are compensations. First that the good work now done will be less undone than at present. Next the manure can be more directly dealt with. Instead of leaving it on the Depot for removal by the contractor, and thus naturally at his own time, and by his own men, not under direct corporation control; would it not be better for the Corporation to deliver directly to those who use the manure? Such cultivation might be dealt with collectively, thus forming, so far at least, the beginnings of an Agricultural Co-operative Society. Its members would thus get their share of manure in such quantities, and at such regular times, as could be arranged. For the Municipal Cleansing Inspectors would have their list, and their carters would soon get into the habit of following it. In this way the present local dumping, into "depots", which are too much mere centres of nuisance—and worse, even infection, from dust, flies &c.—would be got rid of: and good work done daily would no longer be so much undone as at present.

This proposed method is undeniably more expensive to the Corporation: but on the other hand, it can fairly charge for its manure

whatever price the cultivators are at present paying to the contractor, (at any rate till the initial extra expenses are met). In this way there will be some increased income towards balancing the extra outlay; and this can easily be computed.

It is a difficulty, for every Municipality, that the large number of carts and carters required for early and prompt removal of dirt are not in use for a sufficiently long period of the day. But here in very many of the 821 Kholas, and in other places besides, are positive quarries of manurial matter for pasture, which will largely have to be carted out some day; and the sooner this is begun the better for the city's improvement. Despite old bricks and sticks, (which also have their value) this rubbish is more valuable than it looks: its old lime for instance is of value, as well as the nitrogenous, phosphatic and other manurial substance which it will yield the soil.

Nothing excites greater dislike in India than the use of night-soil in agriculture; but this is explained by the unskilled treatment of it, sometimes by cultivators, but above all in "trenching grounds." These are a nuisance in too many cities; but merely where more manure is put into the earth than it can sanitate. Applied in moderation, and well covered with earth, there is no nuisance whatever, no smell perceptible by the keenest nose: and soon all melts together into a rich soil, invaluable for crops. To this care and proper treatment of all waste matter, the extraordinary fertility of China is very largely due: and conversely, the ever increasing poverty of Indian agriculture and horticulture is inevitable, while cattle-manure and leaves are burned as fuel (in the prevalent neglect of tree-planting), and while Municipalities, and their city public also, fail in the agricultural economy, and therefore social duty, of retnrning all this waste matter to the soil.

Whitewashing and its Incentive to further Improvements.

Of all the cleaning and brightening of Patiala City for the recent visit of the Prince of Wales, the extensive Whitewashing and Coloring along the main line of streets has been the most conspicuous and enduring, and thus the most encouraging and hopeful, towards the present thoroughgoing scheme of City improvement.

For this sudden and dramatic change of scene cannot but have caught the public eye: and it is gratifying to find the example being already followed throughout the city here and there, and by small houses as well as large. But these are too few for adequate example to their neighbourhoods; whieh are moreover a little demoralised in this matter, by the fact that the recent washing was done wholesale and in haste, and thus at State expense. No State or Municipality, however paternal, can be expected to wash up for all its citizens; but now is the time for public announcement that it is now the turn of the citizens to wash up for themselves, and for the credit of the City, and State also, and as example to the provincial towns as well. Still, to give this useful nd stimulating activity a fresh start, and now that this season's rains are over, may I submit the suggestion that it be publicly announced (1) that this recent whitewashing is intended as an example to the city generally, but that it be done by the citizens at their own expense, as improving their own property, and this even in material value. But also (2) that to encourage any who may feel this moderate expense a difficulty, the Municipality will provide the loan of brushes, ladders, etc., without charge, and will also see to the supply of the whitewash (and coloured wash to the house-holder's desire) of good quality and at cost price. Also (3) workmen may be provided, through the Municipality who, by larger contract, (and perhaps too with organising assistance from the Registrar of Co-operative Societies) may thus save the householders the trouble of separate contracts, and this with economy as well.

I trust it is not too much to hope that the members of the Municipal Council may themselves take a personal interest in thus stimulating their respective wards. The inspectors and other officers of the Municipality will thus be not a little helped and encouraged in the propaganda.

Finally may not Municipal garlands (and Samadhs perhaps as well) be promised to the best coloured houses ?—as also to the best Mistri and workmen ? By this simple and inexpensive device, a real stimulus, and for next year's improvements too, will be given.

There are some, and even among sanitarians, who say of such proposals.—All this is but superficial : more substantial improvements are needed ; so let us do them first. But from life-long experience of city improvements, and these largely in slum quarters of which Patiala has happily no idea, I can testify that no stimulus to general repair and improvement is so widely and rapidly efficacious as this broadside discharge against dirt, and of its depressing gloom. So by all means let this new wave of whitewash be not general in particular streets, or even lanes, unless where all so desire. Much better let the bright house tell its own tale, and persuade its neighbours by showing them their disadvantage. The women's and children's appreciation of even a single brightened house in their neighbourhood will often bring about the same change of their own homes, in the next year, or that following.

Beauty of Old Houses.

Of course many houses have external paintings, though often fading, and these should be encouraged too, as by special awards of garlands and praise.

Moreover there are many fine old red brick fronts in Patiala which never have been coloured, and do not need to be. Here pointing, (of the spaces between bricks from which mortar has fallen) is sufficient, with repair and painting of wood-work, etc , where necessary.

For the improvement of housing conditions in Patiala, and thus of house-values, we need to revive the old "*house-pride*" which so often inspired their building and dignified their occupancy. This is now too much forgotten in the general depression and dinginess, which no doubt came in with the fall of population from disease ravages after the 1900 Census. Well, now is the time for the reverse wave, the returning fashion. For the present moment of dread of wholesale demolitions, which the visit of the town-planner inspires here, (as at first sight in every city) will soon be replaced by the common-sense understanding, and, I trust, the approval of the present scheme—with (*a*) its extremely few proposed demolitions, and these only where positively necessary for the public good, and of course with fair and full compensation, and careful attention to replacement ; and (*b*) its general and detailed improvements towards the health, convenience, and prosperity of the city, its recreation and pleasure, its widely enhanced beauty also.

Thus arises the time, in fact "the psychological moment"—for the active encouragement of the citizens to bear their part in this general improvement, and this not only in their own interest, in that of their neighbourhood, and even of the whole city, but also for its position and example throughout the State, and its credit among Punjab and Indian capitals generally. Men do not shrink from following their Prince to war ; they find their pride and even joy in facing its risks and sacrifices accordingly : why then, when the like lead is given in peace and towards the public weal, need they, or their fathers either, be doubted ?

True it is, alas, that a peace campaign does not suddenly stir the blood like those of war ; and old habits, shortsighted economy, and, worst of all, current apathy and indifference, make public arousal far more difficult. But hence all the more necessity for beginning with such simple and inexpensive, yet conspicuous and rapidly convincing and diffusing improvements as those which such a "*Brightening-up-Movement*" produces. And of this I have had ample evidence, and in East and West alike. Thus, what promised only to be a temporary and local association of this kind in Dublin slums around the Town-Planning Exhibition of 1914, not only brightened up eleven streets that season, but has worked on through all the subsequent and peculiarly troubled eight years since then, and with the resolve not to dissolve until the whole 1100 streets of the city are dealt with.

Proposed Exhibition of Photographs, Sketches, etc.

Last New Year I found an artist sketching in Patiala, and full of delight over its beautiful old houses ; and now my assistant has made some sketches in his turn. But a whole series of photographs needs to be made, and at many points throughout the town ; and thus it is possible soon to hold a small Exhibition. This would disclose to many eyes the too much forgotten fact that Patiala is far richer in interest and even beauty than is at present realised. For here is much of excellent architectural design, with admirably skilled brick-work, with doors too of remarkable workmanship, and set in carving exquisitely wrought. Could I transport one of these old house-fronts to Europe, the greatest Museum would gladly give it a place of honour in its Architectural Hall. For though narrow streets and lanes were inevitable here in their day, as in other old fortified cities, these old householders and their mistris have created between them homes by the hundred which only art and love can build. To open people's eyes anew to this heritage, individual and public alike, is necessary, and such a little Exhibition will make it practicable.

These good traditions of the building crafts are not yet wholly lost amid the vulgarised Western imitations too common in recent work. It only needs appreciation and encouragement to renew them Mere imitation of the past work is not asked for; but with recovered respect for this, Patiala will have a style of its own again. Of internal decoration I cannot speak, but the fame of that of the Shish Mahal, etc., has reached me; and it was presumably decorated by local artists who no doubt have also left their mark in city houses. Western fashions no doubt at present predominate in India; but the revival of Indian art is manifest, in Calcutta especially, and also elsewhere. The Punjab too will soon have its renewal; and the mistris of Patiala are worth encouraging towards share in this.

Further Social and Civic Results.

This renewal of "house-pride" will also serve the revival of "health-conscience"—two ideas which return together; and which deliver all who grasp them from the too frequent delusions (1) that wealth is a personal matter of money, instead of real family well-being; (2) that health is a matter of individual chance, instead of domestic and public care.

How to advance these more readily, so that the householder shall be encouraged to set his house in thorough order of repair and health, within as well as without, and of seemliness accordingly? Public opinion needs to be roused and advanced; so here local lectures need to be given, leaflets distributed, etc. But above all is needed here an impulse and encouragement from above, from the State, supported and diffused by the City Authorities and their staff, seconded by such volunteers and auxiliaries as they can gather. Here too Lady Doctors, Teachers, and Nurses can help greatly, with their access to house-mistresses and their daughters.

But along with such propaganda why not the appeal of praise, the award of honour? Why should State and City be mainly thought of as merely punishing offenders? Let them also be realised as appreciating well-doing. Every one must have noticed the big ugly census mark daubed high above house-doors throughout the town: why not now offer a small and pleasing and characteristic mark, (say of the Patiala elephant crest and banner?) to be stencilled upon the wall of any house which satisfies an annual municipal inspection as in goo order, outside and in? Two ranks, first-rate and second-rate, with characteristic colours accordingly, might thus be distinguished: and granted of course, not merely to the *pukka* houses which come up to these standards but to *kucha-pukka*, and even *kucha* as well; for such houses also need encouragement, and will be responsive to it. I plead then that this small and inexpensive suggestion be given a fair trial, say of three years. By that time the community would increasingly see the advantage of attaining such good standards; and it would even have examples of the money advantage, since a house thus recognised can be sold to more advantage than one below first or second level.

CHAPTER IX.

General Planting and Adornment of the City; as (much of) Garden City.

The Baradari Garden.

After enjoying the restful hospitality of the Baradari Garden during my whole stay in Patiala, it would be blind, as well as ungrateful, to fail in recognising its many qualities. For here are the stately drives, the noble trees, the spacious lawns and park views of Western palaces and mansions; yet all worked out with trees and flowers often unfamiliar, and always beautiful.

Still, since brought here as a designer, and therefore so far as critic, it may be pointed out that this scheme—essentially of English gardening—dates from after its best period, and thus does not always reach its best effects, since becoming somewhat dispersive. Moreover the green peace of the English landscape produces a feeling of reserve, which hesitates fully to use the gorgeous colour-resources of the tropics, though the occasional splendid climber or flowering tree has not been forgotten. Indeed later gardeners have introduced more of these, and rightly—witness the scarlet borders of the Mexican Christmas-flower (Poinsettia), or the young avenue of gold mohur, (Poinciana). The excellent double avenue of Cypresses,—already pleasing, and in the next generation to become magnificent—is again a recent feature, and from Moghal monumental gardening. Hence, for our present problems of the City, (1) its Parkway with its many Tobahs, each of which is a park-view waiting development, (2) for the Central Nala Avenue, with its smaller open spaces, yet three Tobahs also, (3) for Temple precincts, (4) for minor Roads, and corners innumerable, the style of design must be distinct from that of the Palace Gardens, excellent as these are.

Municipal Gardening.

First a word of praise of the pleasant and well kept Garden of the Municipal Office, and also of the larger Garden beyond the Nala junction.

A fundamental condition is that of economy; the Municipality can afford but little permanent labour for watering and tending; and thus trees and shrubs must be chosen, which need least care, after the ordinary watering for the first year or years necessary for their establishment. Nor can most of the Tobahs be grassed; though fortunately two or three are low enough for some natural verdure, like Tobah Ragho-Majra.

Furthermore, the effects to be aimed at in the City are not simply of verdure and shade; though at due places we need shade of the deepest, and so put it on plan accordingly. The City too is as fortunate as a Dutch or Belgian one in its great green ring of external Canal Boulevards, over six miles and more in extent, with radiations far beyond; so that with all respect to shisham, mango, and all other fine standard trees, we do not need many more of them in the City. To make Patiala the Garden City which it may now so easily become, we must stir public interest; for without that it cannot fully be made so, and still less kept so. How then create this interest?

Popular Interest in Flowers, etc.

Simply enough, if first of all we observe peoples's existing interests. That child with the gorgeous flower-branch of Forest-flame (Erythrina) or Dhak (Butea) in its season, and that flower-shop with its fragrant blossoms, for temple offerings as well as home brightening, are manifest clues. The white Jasmines in one small garden, the glowing pomegranate in another, even the pink oleander growing by the shop-door, the few pots in the balcony, or hung beside the window,—the railway-creeper on the wall, even the solitary Tulsi plant; here are clues again. See in the neglected Temple Garden, and sometimes its sole survivor—the Arna tree (Crataeva religiosa) as exuberant in blossom as the cherry beloved of Japan, and no less exquisite in its own way also, changing to tender and lovely leafage, and this next lit up by glowing fruit. And for concluding evidence, in gardens or by Mosques, the tall columns and noble heads of the palms, which Linne, the patriarchal father of botany, rightly named and ranked as "Principes"—the very "princes" of all trees.

Here there are starting points for our Garden City beginnings; each plant and all are waiting, mutely pleading for that fuller space and development which they will so richly repay.

Allotments?

Might not an opportunity of this kind be arranged in vacant spaces, and in suburbs—as now in so many Western Cities? And this also in connection with Co-operative Societies, as well as to individuals?

Palms, and their use.

First then,—what of the Palms? This is the tree of victory and fame. So—Princes for the Princes—and with precedence, even before the living, of the ancestral dead, the predecessors, the founder of the Dynasty. So with these let us plant the new avenue to the Samadban from College, as well as line the courtyard within its gate. Also a line of palms around the square of its garden, with a mass of five or seven at its farther corners.

The palm also, as the Moslem's traditional tree, which he has spread from Spain to Malaya, claims its place by the Mosques. First that one extending at Raghomajra Tobah, has space for groups and border. And there to complete these fine elements of the future landscape of the Parkway, a further group of palms is indicated on plan on this Tobah on each side of its south entrance by Parkway, (of course not quite symmetrically placed, nor of equal size, but thereby balancing all the better). Finally for this quarter no more palms, save a group at the far north corner of the farther Tobah, that of the cattle. The space and Park-view between these palm-masses will be improved, as viewed from either end, and will seem extended accordingly.

But when planting new palms, why not the best? Are there not better fruiting varieties available than the common? Forest and Agriculture Departments reply—Certainly, yes!—we ask nothing better, than to introduce them.

But palms at first grow slowly. At some points then, as in the low ground beside Samadhan new Avenue, and also at the Tobah corners, we can put, behind the palms, some quick growing Eucalyptus, which can be cut when these are fairly on their upward way.

Colour Effects Easily Possible.

So far future general effect is provided, but colour is wanted; and as soon as may be. Flowering shrubs soon supply this; and hence should be planted in rich and varied bordering—masses of scarlet, white and blue, of orange and purple; and of each plant two or three, or even more, so as to give effect even at distance. One such border should naturally fringe the Samadhan garden wall; both inside and outside so much the better. And so too for the easterly sloping bank of Tobah Raghomajra, and along the whole border of the opposite level side also: it is but enriching the present hedge-row, and brightening the Musjid wall. The Indian laburnum (Cassia) the Dhak, etc. will grow into minor trees, and so much the better: they are sure to be pruned in blossom time.

The northward cattle Tobah can of course have nothing eatable; but no animal will touch the oleander (Nerium); and the houseowners on the west side may be trusted to water such plants as we can find space for between their doors, for their fine masses of pink and white bloom through many months of the year.

Further Examples of Planting Improvement.

At the odd corners here and there as we go northward, the planter will find space only for a single tree or two, and choose with discretion. Sometimes he will put in a big shade tree, if there be space to rest or play under it. Oftener a flowering tree; or, on a dry bank, a drought-resisting shrub: sometimes the beautiful and free growing Duranta, with its violet flowers, its orange berries; its white variety too; if space allows, a golden Cassia or orange Bignonia as contrast. On very dry slopes, a Dhak-tree will survive better; or even at dryest, blue or golden Agave will hold its own.

We thus come to the Nala Junction, with its two fuel yards to west and east. The latter needs only to be set back in frontage some six yards to admit of road-widening and shrubbery border, say of oleanders; and it will still have space enough within. But the former, as occupying the position central to our meeting of three improved perspectives from south, east and west, must be removed. But say merely to the near corner of Tobah Jhumak Lal, thirty or forty paces west; and thus with no serious disadvantage.

Here on this area, between the uniting Nalas, there is need for as tall a central mass of permanent verdure as may be, and with increasingly stately effect. For this purpose, especially in the small area there is nothing which can compare with a group of Cypresses, closely set. This will need replacement of rubbish by deep soil, specially well enriched; but these conditions are easily realised with trustworthy labour, and easy collection of waste matter from neighbourhood.

Colour now is wanted round this central mass; and there is no better contrast to the dark cypress foliage than of bright leaved as well as golden flowering laburnum, of which therefore here some should be put in, outside the Cypresses, with minor and temporary shrubs, or creepers, or the more permanent Oleander again.

Improvement of Nala-Aspects.

Here too, for further colour and fresh effect, the scheme of swinging wreaths of flowering creepers along the Nala fence, and at intervals across it also, (page 55) should here find its culminating feature, and gayest expression. This can be simply done, by erecting at a mere footpath's distance from the uniting Nalas and from that of the road beside them, a row of posts 10 ft. high and 8 ft. apart, (and with a higher pair in the middle of each of the three sides). Transverse bars at 9, 6, and 3 feet above ground level will then run between. Over this framework purple Bougainvilleas, orange Bignonias, etc. will soon twine and flower; and with due guidance, in alternating levels, a fine range of colour magnificence will be assured after a couple of years.

The Laburnum tree will later flower, and in time the Cypress spires will rise above the whole, making this group monumentally complete. But from the first year's growth of the creepers on their high framework, the effect will be pleasing; and the desired central feature to our road junction will thus not have to be long waited for.

The adornment of the Central Nala is even more easy, and inexpensively done. Enough here to supply, in addition to shade and flower trees in its Tobahs, the occasional Cypress besides its tallest houses, and the planting of sacred trees, (*Arna, Bael, Kadam, etc.*) besides its Temple groups.

Examples for Tobah-Improvement.

We pass therefore westwards from Nala Junction, with Tobah Chait Singh and Tobah Jhumak Lal on left and right. At each of their four extreme corners a palm group will in time be most effective, while bright shrubbery groups in front of these will give speedy results. The grouping should be of course varied from preceding ones; and to save watering, hardy plants like Durantas, Agaves, etc. may be given preference.

Avenue Effects: Example for Law Courts.

But we are now approaching not only the Samania Gate, with the future new suburb suggested to south of it, but the Tehsil and the Law Courts to the north. This latter especially is a fine building, with dignified gateway, great courtyard, and spacious compound, yet at present it seems out of the way. In other cities its dignity has given it an imposing position; how can this drawback be remedied?

Quite simply, and yet most effectively, by a long and dignified Avenue; and for this purpose again there is no tree better than the sober and stately Cypress. Between the Tobahs there is space for quadruple row, by planting on each side of the Nala, yet without concealing the corner palm groups and park effect of the Tobahs behind Where the road turns northward towards the Tehsil, an ordinary siugle avenue will suffice, and thence up to the Law Courts' gate; whence it may also be continued by the side road to the Samania Road. As these trees grow, we shall thus have an increasingly fine and characteristic avenue from the Central Nala group we have above been scheming: and thus practically the Law Courts will be freed from their present aspect of isolation, and with their long entrance colonnade of avenue beginning at what is almost the centre of the whole town-plan.

CHAPTER X.

Proposed Central Parkway.

Origin of Parkways and their Advantages.

From the recent remarkable rise of the Town-Planning Movement throughout the United States, an idea has emerged, of the highest value for Cities everywhere. Hitherto, in all cities more or less, their Parks and Public Gardens have been, and as yet usually remain, quite dissociated; and are thus but like oases in the City, otherwise a desert, since it is absence of vegetation which characterises this. But now the American Planners are designing, and their Municipalities are actively carrying out, that most admirable of City Improvements, which they have termed "Parkways." These are not mere ordinary Avenues or Boulevards; but definite connections between Park and Park, and these not simply avenued in the usual way, but also utilising every available vacant space, for small gardens or even for clump planting, of decorative shrubs with patches of flowers: and even planting a tree, however independently of the formal avenue line, wherever an opportunity offers.

In this way the effect of the Public Park or Garden is continued outside its gates, and through its course to the next Park, so that at well-nigh every point of view along the way there is at least a glimpse of verdure or colour: and an attractive call to follow its course farther, and towards the Park at either end. Attractive drives as well as walks are thus created: and as this kind of improvement can most easily be carried out through quarters thinly populated, and of inferior value and aspect, they are carried out more cheaply, and often quite without the costly demolitions which might be required in more expensive and built-up quarters. Thus too the whole neighbourhoods, which they traverse, become improved, and rise in value: so that this class of improvement pays. Again these inferior neighbourhoods were formerly a barrier against city development around them: but thanks to this new and attractive thoroughfare they also develop; again with substantial increase of good building and increased values to the Town.

Practicability in Patiala.

How far is this class of improvement practicable in Patiala? Peculiarly so: most extensively and most easily perhaps of all the fifty cities and more with which I have had to do in India. For here is the peculiar case of a low-lying city long limited by its many Tobah Tanks and the Nalas connecting these: and though it is now a good many years, since the thoroughgoing operations of R. B. Ganga Ram, which filled up the Tobahs and which provided the present well-built Nala courses, these Nalas still practically remain in peoples' minds and habits as outlying boundaries, beyond which the normal extension of good buildings has not yet sufficiently taken place.

It is the one limitation of this well-planned and well-executed scheme that it was so strictly from the Engineering point of view, and did not also include that of Town-Planning, then hardly thought of in India. The result is that the new Roads which accompany the improved Nalas, and which were of course the result of clearances doubtless of considerable aggregate expense, were not at the time carried a little broader, so as to afford a wider and more attractive Avenue if not Boulevard character. It would now be too costly to widen these further to any great extent, save where actually passing through vacant spaces, like old Tobahs; while the Nala beside the course of the new roads, despite its excellent building, cannot be considered attractive.

Yet if this long course of Nala Roads be now inexpensively improved, on Parkway principles, as I now propose to show, we shall thus have a new and even beautiful Parkway system, traversing the City in two directions; and also linking the Moti Bagh and College quarter with that of the Ijlas-i-Khas and the Mall and Baradari—thus a Parkway throughout Patiala from end to end; and well-nigh across also —of course with appreciation of city values accordingly

Hence then the detailed recommendations which follow ; and which tend to make these as yet comparatively outlying Nala Roads into a truly Central Parkway System.

Central Parkway up to Tobah Raghomajra, and Northwards.

Returning now and for the last time to the drive from Moti Bagh past the College, and coming past the Nala junction, we here turn northwards beside the main Nala, planting trees on each side and in irregular corners as we proceed, and thus soon cross the Samania Bazar. Here a fine view opens for the Tobah Raghomajra before us, despite its low lying position and bad character for occasional floodings, is thereby all the greener ; and it is moreover the largest park-space we can have in the whole city. The surrounding houses on our right stand well above it, and a path with shrubbery planting may be made most, if not all, the way upon this sloping bank. The left hand side of this big Tobah has been partly taken into cultivation, partly built on, and the present large additions to the mosque make this a good feature, which a few palms would perfect.

Here then our northward drive needs only a little improvements. Primarily the planting of good clumps of trees at the main points, as indicated on plan; with detached trees between. A central Avenue is not here desirable ; there are many avenues already round Patiala, and we shall propose more : but nowhere else can we have this open view; improved into that of a City Park. The playing-space is not appreciably interfered with : for, with all respect to this area as useful Police drill-ground, may not this be found elsewhere ?—and this fairly grassy space improved into a Playing-field, for the young men of the town in the early mornings and evenings, and possibly during the day for the future High School, when its present beginnings are removed from the Sheranwala Gate and from the College, and unified at some more central situation (discussed later—and conveniently at no great distance from here).

Crossing now the main straight road towards the Water Tank by the Qila, a smaller Tobah opens on the left ; and with crowded interest and picturesqueness in the mornings, as gathering-place for many cattle. Here again, with planting at ends and western edge, and also with trees planted next the buildings on the east, a fresh park effect will be produced.

Northward Course: Improvement of Nala.

For nearly a hundred yards the northerly Parkway passes through buildings mostly of no great interest in themselves, but capable of pictureque treatment with flowering trees and climbers in their inter-spaces. Here too, we may recall the plea and the provision made for these splendidly decorative plants made at the Botanic Garden, (page 31) and adopt its method. For here the narrowness of the drive, the largeness of the drain, and the separation it makes from the path beyond, can be given a new unity, and even a fresh and striking effect. The simple device is that of growing climbers, upon the iron fence of the drain, and swinging across the drain, say at every alternate post, a wire to the other side, (coiled over, if need be, with cord) so as to carry a festoon from side to side. Though there is thus no covering of the drain, nor the slightest interference with its cleansing, the effect of the series of these, seen in perspective as we walk or drive, will be of garlanding. This will at once veil the drain as a too prominent feature, and bring together the drive on the one side with the path on the other, so producing the effect of a broad boulevard, and this decorated, indeed as never before or elsewhere.

We have thus a device of the utmost simplicity and inexpensiveness. It admits therefore of extensive use along our way, and with infinite variety from point to point, and changeful interest throughout the seasons. Granting some initial collection of climbers at the Botanic Garden, (as already begun at the Baradari), cuttings, etc., need cost nothing. Little even for planting, or for subsequent care, if picked school boys, as boy scouts, be simply given a little guidance.

After crossing the road from Topkhana, the view again widens over a Tobah on each side, that on the right largely cultivated, that on the left partly built over. Following the present road, that towards the east, we soon come to opposite the Nala Junction. Its angle is at present occupied by a small fuel-yard with another opposite to the right. Their improvement has been considered above (page 52).

Central Improvement Nala Junction.

Our road now bends to the left and west, and here coincides with that from the Sunami Gate to the Central Nala and between two more Tobahs, (Phil Khana and Jhumak Lal). Here is one of the main crossings of the city, and also the one most open for effective and varied treatment upon our whole range of parks and Parkway from South to North. Yet also inexpensive treatment; for no buildings have to be interfered with, and little other alteration made save the exchange of the present positions of the two small fuel-yards for others at no inconvenient distance. For that in the angle of the Nala Junction the treatment recommended after consideration of various alternatives, is to focus here our decorative scheme of gorgeous climbers, by giving them a twofold or triple fence of varied heights and levels accordingly; while within the enclosed space there will still be room for a group of cypresses, or palms. In this way, a striking effect of verdure and colour can be obtained in three years, or even two; while later there will emerge above this gay and mingled web of climber-grouping, the rising and clustered heads of the central trees increasingly dominating the whole picture and its perspectives for many years to come.

Northward Course, Continued.

This whole group will not only give an effective centre for our present approach, or for that from the Central Nala but also when coming along the Sunami gate road between the two abovenamed Tobahs. For this straight perspective upon this cypress and climber group an Avenue is obviously needed. But as this road should also have open views upon the Tobahs on each side, and as the trees should also have here the most regular and formal character possible, the best effect will be got by planting Cypresses throughout the whole length, after all little over 200 yards. The simple treatment of the Tobahs is shown on plan.

Two farther additions hereabouts are desirable, though they can be left till later. First, coming northward, just below the Junction of the Nalas, a new bridge across the Nalas will admit of a direct drive curving round towards the Chauk Rautan (an important road junction needing slight improvement to be discussed later.) Thence it divides towards (1) the Central Nala, and (2) the Bazar Dharampura, as main road to Sheranwala Gate (as from it to the Qila).

The second of these improvements to this Parkway scheme is afforded by the easy possibility of an oblique and almost direct crossing from this parkwey, a little beyond where it crosses the road from Topkhana, and thence between the kacha house, on the left (with little damage to them), and so across the Tobah Phil Khana to cross the Sunami Road at its oblique angle. (This can be done without disturbing the small pakka house at the N. W. angle of the Tobah. Though it is rather a pity that it is there, it can be improved by small flowering trees.)

Starting now northwards anew from this angle, and crossing of Sunami Gate Road, we have a northward stretch with the fairly open Band School Compound on the west. We thus soon come to the Tobah Chet Singh, already fully planted as the Municipal Garden, and with a fine Temple to N. W. of this standing in another small old Tobah, which had better be filled up (at least unless some unexpected pious donor be willing to deepen it into an orderly temple tank,) The other small Tobah opposite the municipal garden is lying desert; but it can be easily improved as usual, with a little planting as shown on plan.

Corn Market Quarter.

The Parkway now crosses the Corn Market (Bazar Anajmandi) and soon reaches Dhobi Ghat Tobah on the right, a long perspective easily beautified, as is also the portion of Tobah Anajmandi on the west. With this our long series of Tobahs so named, (no less than eleven so far in all) comes nearly to an end; though not yet the series of park views, or of associated avenue and street vistas.

For we soon come past the irregular and easily beautified edge of Dhobi Ghat Tobah on the east, and similarly of mostly large houses on the west, and come to open views again. First on the left comes in the Nala Kanerian, with a low lying garden to north of it (which can easily here spare a few feet, say 10 at most, for road-widening.) We now emerge upon a larger view, that of the large and low Park space in front of the Government Offices (Ijlas-i-Khas) which is obviously the last of the Tobah series, green since low-lying, but now well drained.

Ijlas-i-Khas.

At present we have to drive round to and through the Sheranwala Gate. But to complete this Parkway as it deserves, and not lose this final Parkview, is easily effected by continuing by the present walk above the small Nala. This needs only a little lowering and levelling, to make it one of the most effective sections of the Parkway coming northwards.

For we thus see the fine range of the Government Buildings at their best. Yet this best admits of two slight enhancements. First by pruning down the too great massiveness of the clump of trees, which has grown up so large and high as practically to conceal the unity of the buildings, and break them asunder in to two separate masses. Secondly, the buildings from here look too low. Yet they can immediately be given a striking addition of apparent height, and corresponding dignity, by the simple and inexpensive expedient of (*a*) smoothing into a terrace the untidy and sloping bank of the park area above which they stand, and (*b*) running a straight regular footpath along the base of this terrace. This path should (*c*) be covered with red brick-dust, which will harmonise with the pleasing colour scheme of the buildings. It thus affords a further improvement of this new base-line for them, with increased effect of height, proportion, and dignity accordingly.

The Mall and Conclusion.

Now, passing the Sheranwala Gate and these Government Offices, we have reached the spacious and regular Mall, which connects the two main long Boulevard ranges, which on both west and easterly sides so handsomely enclose the entire City. We are also on the line of entrances to the spacious, even magnificent Baradari Park, and again with its surrounding Avenues. But now, instead of the City lying, as it has hitherto done, so bare and treeless between the Palace Parks to the north and south respectively, it is surely a substantial gain to the amenity of the City, and even to the Palace Parks themselves, thus to convert this long neglected Drainway into a Parkway, and this of a peculiarly varied and interesting character.

Between the city streets and the external Boulevards, here is an intermediate drive; one full of varied interest and picturesqueness as its simple planting develops (as it so speedily can do, through use of climbers before the trees have grown to height and flower.) Though a couple of miles in length, the expenses on estimating will be found surprisingly small; since,—given the excellent engineering of the scheme due to Rai Bahadur Ganga Ram some good few years ago—we have had little to do, save to add this ornamental planting, which transmutes a Drainway hitherto avoided, into what may soon become the most attractive feature of the City, its Central Parkway.

CHAPTER XI.

Transverse Avenues, in North of City.

The Mall, and Hospital Tank.

Leaving the interior of the Baradari, already so fine at many points, for such further improvements as may arise in the skilled hands of Mr. Burrows, we pass along the Mall eastwards; as First Avenue in this direction. Slight changes would greatly improve the large Daviji Temple area and its effects, but these we leave to the later chapter dealing with sacred buildings. The well-made banks of the great Hospital Tank need only a patch of overhanging trees to veil its too sharp and narrow N. W. angle, and another at the bend besides the adjacent Temple Tank.

King Edward Statue.

The island-slopes around the pedestal of the King Edward Statue are however at present left somewhat too stiff and formal, and need verdure--not of course any trees, but simply shrubbery of the lowest growth, say the roses of England around the pedestal, and the jasmines of India next the water. For these will gracefully droop towards it in soft and rounded masses; and thus greatly improve, indeed bring out, the effectiveness both of the sculptor's and the architect's design.

Beyond a few more flowering shrubs to brighten the Mall front of the Hospital, the road to the Lahore Gate, and the Mall front of the Orphanage also, we reach the Canal and its Boulevards, and cross to the Station without need of further suggestions. The Station building too is seemly enough, and the Dak Bungalow and Indian Guest House are increasingly pleasing in aspect and effect.

Second Avenue—(Canal Boulevard to Sheranwala Gate, etc.)

Now turning southward by the main Canal Boulevard, we may best take the first turn westwards, thus practically entering the city; since we thus soon come to the Lahori Gate by either of the two westerly roads on each side of the irrigation stream. Already this gives pleasing pictures, and with better buildings (though still small ones), and such planting as space allows, we have the beginning of a new and second Avenue, broadly parallel to the Mall, and in contrast to it, since now varied and informal instead of regular. This road we may continue, with slight plantings to give it more attractiveness, past the cultivated field south of the great Tank, onwards across the Sheranwala Gate Road, and thence downwards by its little Nala, till we meet the Parkway, with which its whole range is now continuous,—an obvious mutual improvement, needing only a little tidying and planting for its completion. Furthermore, a rough continuation track is already in existence further westward, needing only a bridge over the Nala, with metalling and planting, to give us a seemly Avenue connecting that coming down southward from the main Ring Boulevard, immediately west of the Government Offices Garden. Finally, on plan is shown a slight further continuation of this southward road connecting it (and without any demolition save cutting through a single wall) with the Main Parkway north of Dhobi Ghat.

The preceding minor extensions of the Avenue system are not urgently needed for traffic, though not useless. But when carried out they will appreciably extend that development of much of Patiala to the Garden City level which is the object of this planning.

Third Avenue ("Old Jail Road" improved).

Returning to the Lahori Gate, and entering its Road, the good impression of its long perspective, yet varied aspect, soon gives way to a depressing feeling, from the dilapidation at the entrance to the predominant and overpowering effect of ruin, which, despite a few good houses, is given by "Kholas" without number further on. We postpone these ruins for later discussion (Chapter XXII) and keep to the present and opening problem, that of city amenity. We therefore leave Lahori Road for the present, and take the first turn westwards. For here we have another long line of road broadly parallel to the Mall, Though at present too bare and uninviting, it is broad enough in great part for avenue treatment. It easily admits of further slight widenings, where trees can be introduced. Continuing such only slight demolitions and these mainly of ruins, we soon reach the Sheranwala Bazar, and there see that (at a later stage, as for several preceding minor improvements) it will be possible to get beyond (or through) this, and again join the Parkway.

Coming southwards from the Baradari, and reckoning the Mall outside it as the "First Avenue" of Patiala, that parallel to it, outside the Lahori Gate, is "Second Avenue"; and now this "Third Avenue" continues the series, and now fully within the city, and serving a much larger population accordingly. Not yet very large as compared with the increasing crowding as we look southward; yet, as a direct and seemly avenue—first from Lahori Road to Sheranwala Bazar, and by and by with a little improvement, (in conjunction with the Parkway) to the Corn market street (Anajmandi)—it is of real and increasing value to the city.

And if all this northern region be of lower value and scantier population than elsewhere, all the more are the needs of improvement. And happily the possibilities also, to which we may now turn.

Old Jail Area: Proposed Improvement.

In every city the Jail creates an unattractive neighbourhood for free citizens; and this character tends long to survive the removal of the Jail to country quarters. Nor can this locality be substantially improved while the popular dislike is maintained, as undoubtedly it is, by the detention of the Criminal Tribe within a portion of these walls. First then, for city improvement's sake, I must plead for their removal and this outside the city altogether. As further argument for this, the various experiences of reforming such people elsewhere in India, and indeed in the Punjab in various points, convincingly show that this is best accomplished in well chosen rural surroundings, and under effective moral and social guidance, both agricultural and industrial—however also accompanied, while necessary, by the forces of external supervision and restraint. Assuming these propositions, the planning of this area may be proceeded with, though its execution must await this removal. Productive planning moreover will furnish a fresh argument for this, as of obvious economic return, (1) from surrounding property appreciated in value, and (2) from excellent sites, meantime vacant, but waiting to be utilised.

The full proposal will be at once understood by reference to the plan. It centres from the fine and lofty frontage of the surviving Jail building, which despite dilapidations behind, will reward repair and preservation, if use can be found for it.

Proposed New Municipal Office.

It is manifest that the present Municipal Office is too small for the evergrowing needs of the City, and that substantial extensions are required, practically involving either large rebuilding upon the present site, or removal to another. I recommend the latter course, and this Jail site as the best available. Though in the same quarter of the city, the objection at once arises of inferior accessibility; but this, as the plan shows, is substantially got over. This new situation will be seen (as planned) to be in easy reach of the present situation of the Municipal Office and its main thoroughfare, and also to be in more widely opened contacts with the large surrounding quarters, at present not easily reached from the Municipal Office. The new situation is quieter also, and more favourable for office work; and while becoming even more widely accessible, it will abate the trifling interruptions which arise more readily on the main thoroughfare.

New Residential Quarter.

Furthermore, as will be seen as the plan is studied, the surrounding development of a new residential quarter, and this one of the most attractive which the limited area of Patiala City can offer, will be at once aided by thus centring upon a fine public building. Municipal officials may readily take up some of the neighbouring sites; and here and there an active Municipal Councillor also. Moreover, given this fine frontage, the necessary additions can be made economically, as simple wings. Fully thirty sites of moderate and varied size are suggested on the present Jail area, and nearly as many on the northward side; but of course there need be no objection to the taking up of more than one such site for a larger dwelling or garden.

Hospital Tank Boulevards.

The essential idea of this planning is the intersection of the present Old Jail Road by a new wide Boulevard, ranging from this fine old architectural frontage, so well worth preserving, and all the way to the fine Hospital Tank, and aligned upon its Island Statue. The resulting effect, of intersecting Boulevards, will not only be the best of the kind obtainable in Patiala, but one not easily matched in many greater capital cities.

The whole scheme involves hardly any demolitions, and these of the slightest values; while it brings into productive use not only the site of the old Jail, but also the open space and adjacent compound, at present merely occupied by the remains of a former railway (mainly now only of scrap-metal value, or at best easily stored elsewhere). The main private property to be acquired between the Old Jail Road (now as "Third Avenue" though deserving a better name than this) and the Second Avenue from Lahori Gate westwards, is without buildings, and is partly more or less cultivated, partly used for fuel stores, which are easily located elsewhere. Finally, the small slip of irrigated land between this Second Avenue and the Tank is cut through, in order to bring the mai n new Avenue from the Jail (say rather the proposed Municipal Office) upto the bund of the Tank. Here carriages will stop and turn, the Bund being obviously reserved as a Promenade.

Hospital Tank Promenade.

This Tank Promenade is closed on the east by the grounds of the Hospital (from which, it will be noticed, the plan suggests acquiring only the very few square yards needed for a neat and regular finish). But westwards it not only runs to the S. W. corner of the Tank (with return thereafter to the Second Avenue), but may be readily continued upon the excellent bund on the west side, upto and past Daviji Temple, and thus to the Mall, and the Baradari entrance Gate.

It is not necessary, or even desirable, to go to the expense of widening or fencing this long Bund Promenade into a driving road. Carriages can easily go round by Sheranwala Gate, as at present.

Proposed Flower Garden and Band-stand.

The acquirement of the whole patch of irrigated land, immediately south of Tank, is recommended for laying out as a Municipal Flower-Garden, with some shade trees also, and seats round them. A simple Band-stand may also be provided, and Music, Indian as well as European, encouraged by turns. A large popular audience can even be accommodated on the vacant space south-west of Tank, and this without eviction of its present partial use by Dhobis, etc. On this open space also an Open-air-Theatre may easily also be constructed, and this with gain to the School Play-ground, since a fresh resource.

Must it not be admitted that Patiala is lacking in such resources of open-air attractiveness and simple pleasures? Nor are such recreative hours without their economic value. The most efficient industries, and even the most strenuous business, are found in communities which have also provided themselves with means of healthy and simple recreation for all classes, and in the open-air especially. This Tank Promenade then, with its improving accesses from various parts of the city, would soon become an appreciable gain to it, and in every way.

Fourth Avenue (South and Old Jail Area.)

Returning now to the Jail,—(New Municipal Office, may I not now call it ?) we have behind this, to the south, a shorter and smaller road parallel to the large avenue to northward, and just broad enough to admit trees, at least during the greater portion of its course. This course runs east to Lahori Road with a little (but very inexpensive) cutting; and also west, with a very little cutting also, past the small Tobah Kashmirian. This also is shown simply improved into a little park or rather Playground, with a few shadetrees, and with access from the lanes to south and south-east, also inexpensively obtained. We thus come out near the bend of the Bazar Sheranwala into the Bazar Dharampura—a double corner needing the two slight alterations indicated on plan, which will much abate liability to accidents, and at small expense.

The road congestion at this point is however further dealt with, and in two ways, larger and smaller, which can be taken up as funds allow. The smaller is of further improving communication between the present Municipal Building site and its thoroughfare, and the proposed new site and area, by widening the lane opposite the present Municipal Garden into a new short street. This can be done by sacrificing half of a single one-storey block. This will also somewhat lighten congestion at the neighbouring bend, connecting the main streets.

The larger scheme is to continue Sheranwala Bazar in straight line southwards into Chah Mughlan; and thus can be done to a sufficient breadth with moderate setting back of several housefronts on the way. We thus also improve access to and from the long east and west thoroughfare (which we might now almost call the Fifth Avenue, were it wide enough for planting, which it only is at intervals), as shown on plan. With slight improvements, this useful route—from far west of Takia Rahimshah, and by M. Nun Garan to Water Tank B, and thence to the large open space of Tobah Mul Chand, not far from its conspicuous Arya Samaj Building—can be made more passable for vehicles, and thus of greater value. For Kholas (ruins) may be set back, to provide "sidings" for vehicles to pass, so that other setting-back may be left for rebuilding, as this gradually proceeds. With the cutting of a single pukka building, this road can also be more speedily opened out.

Bhupinder Press Road.

The Bhupinder Press Road, shown on plan as avenued throughout the greater part of its course, may easily be widened to completeness at its southern end, where it enters the Tobah Mul Chand, which has so often been suggested as a small park area, though never finished.

CHAPTER XII.

Improved City "Eastern Park" Entrance.

Tobah Mul Chand and Tobah Pirthinath.

We have here two kindred areas, on opposite sides of Lahori Road, and the first named the larger. They should however, for planning purposes, be viewed together and as part of a main access to the city from the large Canal Boulevard on the east, so that many conveniently enter here coming from the Railway Station, and thus obtain their first impression of Patiala City. It will be seen that the present planning (again without a single demolition, save of ruins, and few even of these) gives this a pleasing and favourable aspect. The Pirthinath Tobah is shown as regularised on both sides, with its wide and vacant street to north planted, and thus giving a Vista of some extent while improving the adjacent properties. Play-ground facilities for its neighbourhood are thus improved also.

The larger Tobah is little altered, save that the Bhupindra Press Road—since destined to much increased importance from the above Old Jail Site improvement scheme—is shown carried straight on through its west end, and past the back of the Arya Samaj building. The small section cut off is proposed to be raised 2, or 2½ feet, like the ground round the Arya Samaj building. This can easily be done with some of the only too abundant rubbish disgorged from the Lahori Gate Kholas, using that of some soil value, (as it so largely has from sweeper's deposits these many years past). This little terrace or platform needs of course a retaining wall, easily built of the many waste bricks of the neighbourhood, though needing good mortar, and cement at top. On this, with little hollows easily watered, should be planted a row of shadetrees, conveniently Pipals, as soonest started with only a year or two of watering, and also as congenial on a public place marked by two of the leading Hindu buildings of the City. This terrace of shadetrees, with seats between, would soon become a pleasing resort: and Music might also here be encouraged, as Sports upon the level ground in front. With the few other trees indicated on plan, we can thus readily complete this Eastern Park Entrance to Patiala.

Further Street Improvements Southwards.

Beside the Arya Samaj building we have the convergence of two roads into the central bazar town, viz. that from Station or from Lahori Road, and that from Bhupindra Press, as well as minor lanes. Some widening is here required. But cutting away pukka buildings is too expensive, and can be avoided. For all that is positively needed, it will suffice (1) to take into the street the sites of three small one-storey shops facing east to the little temple, and also (2) to set back the (at present very untidy) row of one-storey shops as shown on plan. We have thus a public place, seemly and spacious. From this we may in time somewhat improve the Alipurian street as shown on plan. But more satisfactorily, we proceed, without any further alterations, down the long, respectable and much used Katra Sahib Singh Bazar, past the well-known Tirbani, and thence straight on to Safabadi Bazar, not far from its City Gate.

CHAPTER XIII.

Central Nala as Central Boulevard.

Central Nala.

Coming southwards past Tirbani, the first turn on the right and eastwards is well marked by the beginning of the long brick Central Nala crossing the town, and hitherto practically dividing it into two separate halves. This long continued evil needs abatement; and this by nothing short of developing it (as Nature has been indicating from the first) into the Central Boulevard of the city. Such additional openings, to and from each side, as can be inexpensively effected, will be found well worth providing.

This seems a large programme; but it is much less difficult or costly than may appear at first sight. Entering upon it from the east end, the entrance seems unpromising; but it only needs the removal of the tottering wall of the Khola on the left to show the considerable expanse and obvious possibilities of the fairly large Tobah Imdadali. This may be simply yet advantageously developed, as shown on plan.

Improvement of Temple, (and of other Temples).

Proceeding westwards along the Central Nala next comes in view the foreground feature, of a little Temple among its flowers. But this temple needs some repair and re-colouring, and the wall (somewhat unnecessarily high) is all but ruinous. Now returning to the Sanatan Dharam Sabha, whose neighbouring open space we have so lately, as above, been planning to improve, may we not ask this, as one of the leading groups of the Hindu Community, whether it may not be possible to arouse a wave of interest in this neighbourhood, and indeed throughout the city generally, towards the repair and re-colouring of as many of the Temples as may be? Towards the planting of sacred trees, where necessary, and of temple flowers where possible? It is not necessary to belong to the Hindu faith to appreciate how much of the beauty of Indian cities and streets is due to their many Temples, great and small; and also to see, as from outside one cannot help seeing, that if their neglect and deterioration be partly due to a diminished visiting of them, this is also unduly helped by their fading attractiveness. Widely though the religious buildings of the world differ according to their particular faiths, they none the less all agree in the great service of refreshing the human spirit, and this by peace within the sacred enclosure, and by its beauty from without. Why then should not the members of any, and every, historic faith—even though as often in these days becoming less dogmatic in their convictions, and less regular in their practices—conserve and maintain, even from historic pride, from ancestral tradition, and also from actual citizenship, this great heritage of ancestral piety, and of its Sacred Art? Assuredly to those of stronger convictions this conservation makes a yet more urgent appeal. And that the present indifference is but temporary, is evidenced by the increasing respect for old and sacred buildings, with corresponding energy and devotion, generosity, and even sacrifice, towards their repair, which is now manifest in so many cities, of East and West alike ; and nowhere more than at Amritsar, not far away.

In my previous town-plannings, as notably at Lucknow, no co-operation has been more gratifying than that with various Temple authorities, as regards their buildings, sacred trees, and flower gardens ; and such improvements are also appreciated by city authorities, as by the neighbourhoods to which they thus give example and stimulus to more general ones. In such matters local initiative is needed, and surely here should not be too difficult to set agoing.

Mosques, Imambaras, &c.

While on the subject of religious buildings, and as two Mosques in the present neighbourhood also come into view, a word of appreciation also of this form of architectural beauty is necessary. May it also carry with it a plea for the planting of their characteristic and sacred tree in all the countries through which Islam has spread, the noble datepalm, with its perfect harmony, yet contrast, with domes and minarets ? And as at least two Mosques have been lately in building or repair in Patiala, and a third at Tobah Raghomajra is in process of large and fine extension of its buildings, this time of pleading for such completion, by palm-planting, is surely a hopeful one.

Mohalla Mir Kundila ; Proposed Garden Court or Sahan between Mosque and Imambara.

At present an unsightly ruin separates these two sacred buildings. If this ruin were levelled the resulting Open Space would enhance their dignity ; still more if planted with palms or cypresses and flowering shrubs. The south side of this proposed space or garden court is at present occupied by a small kutcha-pukka house in a somewhat tumble down condition. Behind this again is another ruin. Their two sites, if thrown into one, would make one good building site, worthier of the neighbouring pukka buildings.—(See plan herewith.)

This whole improvement is one more example of what may be done by citizens of public spirit to beautify their own Mohallas. It would also be an excellent initiative by the Moslem community.

Gurdwaras.

Along this Central Boulevard no less than three Gurdwaras are conspicuous ; yet, architecturally speaking, hardly conspicuous enough. With all due appreciation of the simplicity of doctrine and life for which these stand, the example of the metropolitan "Golden Temple" of Amritsar is evidence of architectural expression too. And having been fortunate of late years in varied experience of design of religious buildings of the most different types, from the ornate magnificence of the Christian cathedral, and the complex symbolism of the Eastern temple, to the severe simplicity, yet stately unity, of the Jewish meeting place, both great and small, I have clear conviction that the Gurdwara may also have its distinctive austerity and idealism expressed more effectively than in the too simply domestic style into which its architects as yet so commonly fall. Trees too are usually lacking, but I am told that passages in the sacred Granth speak highly of trees, as the shisham and the jujube (Zizyphus) ; so that these are sometimes planted, and with advantage.

Central Boulevard Continued.

Just behind the above mentioned Hindu Temple, on the south side, runs a lane overlooked to the north by a row of tall houses; but the space between this and the Nala road has no building of value; only a small stone-yard and fuel-yard. These are easily located elsewhere; and by this the main road can be widened into an Avenue proper, with its trees planted on the remaining vacant ground on the south, regularised as a low terrace. There is also space for trees at intervals north of the Nala, so a good section of this Central Boulevard is readily made.

Girls' High School: and Proposed New Access.

Of all buildings of importance in Patiala, this is by far the hardest to reach from any other quarter of the city, or to get back from also, as the present Townplan clearly shows. The building itself is good, but its open air-space is very insufficient. A Playground is needed, badly. This can be found to the north, by acquiring the open space with two Kacha houses. An entrance road to a large house intervenes; but as this house has another (and main) entrance from the opposite side, this bit of road may be acquired. Or if this prove too difficult or expensive, a bridge can be made over the one-storey room at the N. W. corner of the school court-yard.

I am told that the old houses opposite the school entrance have long ago been decided on for acquirement, and this will yield housing for the staff, but not much open space nor any improvement of access. But better access is highly important.

This however can readily be obtained from the Central Avenue, past the group of small old Temples, with new large Mandir, and meeting a new entrance easily opened opposite in the School-compound as shown on plan. This long standing difficulty is thus easily and inexpensively solved. Indeed remuneratively, for there will be a very substantial rise of pupils, as soon as the school thus retrieves its bad reputation for inaccessibility, by thus coming out upon the Central Boulevard of the improving City. The accompanying plan shows how much nearer is this access from the southern half of the city also.

The adjacent small open field should also be acquired for the school. Though a few houses at present overlook it, it should be planted along the walls with a double border of mulberry trees, which will serve at once as screen, and as spreading the highly desirable interest of silk-culture among the girls. Furthermore, the present field is used for highly irrigated crops, and is thus complained of, by the neighbours, as a fertile source of mosquito nuisance, and fever accordingly.

Two small new Playgrounds, north and south, are thus provided, and none too much for this large School; the more since little children and big girls need different spaces.

Further access to and from Latourpura and Northwards.

Further access is needed to improve this whole quarter; and by this all its property values will thus be substantially appreciated, by getting into touch with the rest of the town. As first and most striking instance, the long lane north of, and parallel to, the Nala, and ending blindly after over a hundred yards, can be opened out to the Central Avenue a little way west of this new school entrance by merely breaking through a wall, as shown on same plan.

Central Avenue continued to Tobah Mirjan.

The westerly section of this has long been improving; witness the Boys' School building to the south and the adjacent Gurdwara, also on the southern side, with the Tobah Mirjan to northward. The whole only now needs "pulling together," as is shown on plan, to yield satisfactory, and even fine, effect. For this purpose the Tobah Mirjan only needs moderate adjacent planting to north of it, and the wreathing with creepers of its somewhat unattractive railing, to make the two remaining sites (on each side of the big central house now enlarging) more attractive for new houses, which will complete its picture, and enjoy it. The fuel-yard to south is shown slightly set back, to bring out its fine Temple, and thus give a good perspective towards Chauk Rautan. The entrance to this is also widened on the north side of Nala, so giving an avenue entrance and corresponding effect, to the little Park of Tobah Mirjan.

Nala Kashmirian and Street.

This comparatively wide street will reward planting and tidying up. Above all it needs clearing away the unsightly and unhealthy "Sanitary" dump, which spoils its midway open space (obviously an old Tobah); for this street is at present depreciated, and debarred from any possible improvement, by its dirt and smells.

New or widened streets and lanes on the east side show that the Municipal Council has been taking this area in hand; and further improvement will follow continued widening northward, at and beyond the crossing of Takia Rahimshah and M. Nun Garan, and up to Bazar Sheranwala. The value of this improvement is not simply the supply of a direct access from Bazar Sheranwala to Central Nala (or even thence, as we shall see later, to the Qila quarter), but largely also the improvement of communications to and from the whole north central area, at present too much isolated, yet with easy remedies.

CHAPTER XIV.

Chauk Rautan and Corn-Market.

Chauk Rautan: needed widening.

This important convergence of six roads should naturally have been one of the best centres of the whole city and planned with regularity and space accordingly, but it is now too late for anything beyond moderate improvements without undue expense. The accompanying plan shows the utmost which can now be suggested.

First the minor changes:—(a) the widening of approach from Central Nala Avenue; (b) the sacrifice of the two Municipal shops over the Nala, since these obstruct widening. Though in themselves small, they conspicuously spoil the whole perspectives of the junction of the Central Avenue and its continuation to the Parkway. Next, (c) the removal of the small projecting shop at the N. W. corner of Bazar Adalat. So far four one-storey shops in all, for which adjacent reinstalment is easy, as indicated on Plan.

One larger and more expensive widening is however still needed, when funds allow, viz. (d) the setting back of the west side of Chauk Rautan as shown on plan. This is needed to give more space for the considerable traffic to and from the Corn Market (Anajmandi) and also from the road to Law Courts and City entrance (Haveli Kanwarji Sahib street). One pukka house is thus worth acquiring for removal.

Corn-Market (Anajmandi.)

This important street has good breadth in its main northerly portion, but narrows badly towards Chauk Rautan. If possible, three yards of setting back (or at least two yards) should be exacted when plans come up for rebuilding from time to time; but this improvement will be indefinitely slow.

If and when trade increases, and municipal funds admit, the cutting of a new street may justify itself.

Corn-Market and Plague Precautions.

This Corn-Market quarter—with its thoroughly old-fashioned and wasteful ways, (a) of dumping and handling grain upon the street, (b) of showing it upon rough platforms, and (c) storing it in too largely earthen-floored godowns,—has an undesirably established reputation—as such a rat-paradise cannot but have—for the diffusion of plague throughout the neighbouring quarter, and doubtless beyond this as well.

Given the peculiarly terrible plague records of Patiala in former years, and also these permanent conditions for new outbreaks in any season, (besides an annual percentage still most unnecessarily high), it is plainly time to be introducing municipal regulation, which so many other cities are finding of substantial abatement to this most appalling of all the unnecessary and avoidable diseases of India. In Lucknow (for one instance out of many) grain-dealing, with all its indispensableness, is recognised as also a "dangerous trade", and regulated accordingly. The Grainmarkets are thus being strictly localised, with insulation—by demolition when necessary—from surrounding housing; and all shops and stores are required to have pakka platforms in front, and cement or other substantial floors behind, with walls also impenetrable by rats. The result to public health is found to justify this expenditure. Similarly also in Indore City.

Though Patiala City's finances may not yet reach to such thoroughgoing improvement, there is no real hardship in compelling grain dealers to render their floor and walls rat-proof. For it even pays them well to do this, by reducing their present taxation in corn to the rat community, which a little calculation brings out as far more serious individually—and thus to the trade and to the community generally—than is commonly realised.

A range of cement platforms, with raised edges, can be found space for on each side of the wider northern portion of Anajmandi; and, after its construction, the dumping of grain upon the ground (with its inevitable residue for rat-feeding at night) should become, as elsewhere, a municipal offence.

Similar regulation and inspection, should also of course be applied to the grain shops in all other quarters, and to the Seed Bazar halfway between Qila and Samadhan. Indeed, it may safely be predicted that with the rise of health-conscience, which is only as yet in its beginning in cities, the dangerous food trades will be more and more carefully insulated, from their present far too easy infection of the community. Thus a situation like that of the Vegetable Market, (Sabzi Mandi) well detached from neighbouring houses, and fortified by the impenetrable and lofty walls of the Qila on that side, would afford a location for the Seed trade, which would substantially reduce the present risks to the adjacent inhabited quarters.

That no precautions are perfect, especially in populations still far too apathetic in this matter, as to health generally, must be admitted. The keeping of cats is unfortunately not congenial; but the introduction of the beautiful Persian breed, and its patronage by families of rank and education, as increasingly in Europe, would soon have an effect. The loan of rat-traps is practised in some cities, but, with people still so sentimentally merciful as to feel unable to immerse the successful trap in a bucket,—and who therefore let off the rats, to carry death in plague time, to their neighbours—an efficient rat-catcher is needed in each ward of the city, perhaps provided, too, with dog and ferret, and encouraged by payments for results.*

* The type of municipal rat-trap, used here, as by many other Municipalities is expensive, and ineffective after all. Its enormous size makes it inapplicable in most places and above all to animals so highly intelligent as are rats, after the first victim, of which it also retains the persistent smell. Again, mice run in through this too coarse wire meshes; they eat the bait, and defeat the purpose accordingly New and simple traps, for both mice and rats, are therefore required; and it will pay to get them.

And that the public of a city can be substantially stirred up in this matter, and with good results, I can testify from a vivid popularisation of the association of plague with rats and their fleas, which was a feature of our Indore Pageant of Civics and Public Health four years ago, and of which I am lately warmly assured that the lesson is still of continued usefulness throughout the community.

For Malaria too, as an unnecessary mosquito pest (and doubtless for other diseases as well) such popular education and arousal are easily possible. Though still in too slow progress in India, this is going on rapidly in their countries. Thus in Greece, which I remember as frightfully infested, and as apathetically indifferent as can be India, there are now thousands of Malaria Committees throughout the Villages, and with great and ever-increasing results. So here again the high incentive and encouragement not to be despaired of in Patiala could work wonders for public health.

CHAPTER XV.

Bazar Adaulat and Proposed Public Hall. Cinema, Theatre, etc.

Possibilities and Requirements.

This main thoroughfare from Chauk Rautan with its star of roads, and combining their traffic towards the Water Tank and Qila, is fortunately fairly wide. Its buildings are too valuable to admit of further widening without undue expense; hence it will be better to supplement it by the broadly parallel route afforded as far as the Central Nala by the Nala Kashmirian Street and its Northward widening from Bazar Sheranwala (as shown on plan). Leaving this continuation however for the present, this good street, with its many approaches, seems unmistakably the best in the city for the location of what seems one of its main requirements—a good Public Hall, suitable not only for lectures, and meetings, but for entertainments; and of these the most attractive are obviously those of Music, Drama, and Cinema, the present popular favourite. A city of this size can readily furnish paying audiences, and thus attract good films and musical and dramatic companies; and if building were not at present so costly after the War, there might here be a quite legitimate building speculation. To provide such a hall as a Municipal or State enterprise, though quite customary in Continental Europe, is hardly in either Indian or British traditions, which rather look to some generous citizens as pious donor; as in Bombay or Edinburgh, which are thus relatively well supplied, as indeed not infrequently smaller cities also. May it not than be hoped that some donor may also here come forward? Or failing this, that a group of subscribers and guarantors may be formed to construct the building, and assure it from loss for a term of years? Or a combination of both methods, perhaps with some Municipal and State aid as well?

Situation proposed.

The first condition of success for every such building is accessible and conspicuous situation; yet such sites are expensive on the frontage of a main thoroughfare, especially when, as here, purchase and demolition would first be necessary.

Yet we can get over this difficulty, by simply acquiring the good entrance, wide enough for carriages under a conspicuous gateway; if with outlet and gateway upon another adjacent street also, so much the better. This economical method is therefore suggested on plan. The gateways are in Bazar Adaulat and Topkhana Road respectively, (with a private Palace entrance also, from the latter, if desired). The building itself may thus be kept back upon the adjacent Tobah (at present gardened), if testing of this foundation prove satisfactory; or failing that, kept nearer existing buildings. A plain building will thus suffice, since it can be far more cheaply screened with trees and creepers than architecturally elaborated, as it would need to be on the public street. An adequate theatre for an audience of 1,000, can be erected for a sum which, for so desirable a public purpose, should surely be obtainable in ways above suggested.

Utilization of Adjacent Tobah.

The adjacent Tobah may inexpensively be converted into a Public Garden or Playing-field and open-air Gymnasium. An open-air Theatre with space for confectionery and other refreshment-stalls may also be considered.

Possible Co-operation of College, etc.

Finally to give this new recreative centre for Patiala the best possible initiative and guidance, why should not the College take an active share in its management from for the first ? Every history, language, and literature gains by dramatic presentment, by poetical and musical recital, by Cinema as well ; every science has similarly nowadays also its vivid illustration in the Cinema ; so that it is one of the marvels of the conservatism of our Universities that they have not already a "College Cinema" in every city. Yet it is a vivid evidence that they are already in this line of progress that a large proportion of the very best public entertainments of Bombay are held in the Theatre Hall of St. Xavier's College, and largely organised by the students, with only a minimum of supervision by their professors. So here is a precedent of the utmost respectability. The High Schools and the educational community generally will also be reached. This movement is now beginning in American universities and cities.

Conditions of Economic Stability with Cultural Development.

This mode of increasing audiences and maintaining them regularly, from Schools as well as College, and thus from parents and families—in fact thus the bulk of city—is also well worth considering, as a means of making the Hall undertaking in general pay its way from the outset :

and also of attracting to Patiala the best class of entertainments, which at present mainly pass along the main Railway lines not far off.

With the further help of Court interest and patronage, there is no reason why Patiala should not thus share in much of the best at present to be seen in larger or wealthier Cities, like Lahore and Simla. In short we thus see the possibilities of economic stability and of cultural development together.

CHAPTER XVI.

New High School.

Situation and Buildings ?

Since the buildings and the equipments of the present City High School are no longer sufficient, I understand it to be decided that a new High School is to be erected, leaving the present School for junior use. Furthermore, the College is being obliged to recall its present school accommodation to its own uses; and in the first chapter of this Report we have seen that even with the coming extensions, there will be no room for a High School, which must therefore find a new and sufficiently large area elsewhere.

Economy and efficiency thus alike suggest that these coming removals should both be to a single and unified High School; and this therefore conveniently in a more central position, and easily accessible from all parts of the city. Yet outside its crowded areas; and, most desirably, within moderate distance of the College.

The first idea is naturally to find such a site, and to build an entirely new school upon it. But even if the two or three lakhs which can so easily be spent upon such new buildings may be immediately available, it has also to be frankly recognised that the type and planning of Schools, even these at present being built in India, are not adequate to modern requirements, and in fact out of date from the very outset. For as yet even new buildings are mainly conditioned by the too bookish instruction of the past; and this is inevitably more or less reduced to the predominance of cram by the outworn examination system, now rapidly approaching its funeral pyre. which has been too long delayed.

The Current Revival of Education.

Better methods of education are now rapidly coming towards recognition, and even towards replacement of existing ones; in all countries of Europe, and still more in America; and their beginnings are also struggling forward in India. And though no specific type of planning has yet arisen to replace the traditional one, it is already plain that-at all levels, from Madame Montessori's infants, and the less famous, but even more numerous new schools which have been arising throughout the past generation, and increasingly since the War—their main requirement is not of the formal desks and benches and conventional class rooms of the present and passing order of instruction—one essentially of verbalistic empaperment and "Parrot's Training," from "the three R's" up to University degrees, too much alike. The new education, and at all levels has to be of "the three H's":—Heart, Hand, and Head in process of development and guidance together; moral, practical and intellectual in one; and longer withered into so many separate "subjects," but unified in every day's progress, in each scholar's corporate and individual life. Life, that is, of growing kindliness and usefulness, of many practical activities, each and all leading to higher and higher intellectual attainments accordingly; and guided by wise teachers, themselves kindly and skilful, and thus more intelligent in arts and sciences, and far more vital and more interesting in their literary and humanistic teaching accordingly. It is commonly said that such teachers are still too few, and far to seek: but this is explained by the continued survival of Normal Schools of the type established in England after its compulsory Education Act of 1870: which, despite good intentions of its would-be utilitarian projectors, has proved one of the most futilitarian and depressing measures in educational history. With the guidance of effectively modern Professors of Education, Universities are increasingly seeing the need of taking over the instruction of teachers as one of their most important Faculties; and it is thoroughly within the possibilities of Mohindra College with its excellent and progressive Principal and staff—thus moderately recruited—to play a great and vital part in this advance; and not only for Patiala, or even in the Punjab, and its University, but even in India and the world.

For though the past (and too much surviving) Public Instruction System has mainly been towards clerkships or the law—and towards failure and disappointment outside these overcrowded occupations, with infinite waste of young life, and State's and parent's money, and of social productivity when all is done—the nascent revival of education in the best and fullest senses, alike old and new, is towards all directions and occupations, rural and urban alike; and these of course at all levels, of real and increasing efficiency, from humblest to highest service in the community. The present immense proportion of school and college (examination) "failures", too largely continued through their bitter discouragement, and far exaggerated discredit, into more or less of failure in life (or at least of diminished courage and self-respect) is, by the new education, increasingly reduced. And thus its survival is assured: its general acceptance and application cannot be delayed much longer.

Suggested Economy of Location and Development.

Instead then of at once building a New High School, at great expense—and old fashioned from the beginning, as it yet can hardly help being—why not simply seek out some large and conveniently situated old house with ample grounds? This will be less expensive, yet far better serve as the starting-point of gradual developments; as educational ideas and ideals grow clearer, and means of realising them become available, not only through money, but through men.

Such a house will easily afford the requisite shelter from the elements. Larger rooms can be provided by opening out existing partitions. Extensions are easily made upon existing blank walls, or separately as part of a fresh courtyard. Laboratories and workshops can be cheaply erected. Indeed these even entirely by the boys, with only the leadership of a skilled mistri of each craft: as I can bear personal witness from some of the best equipped and efficient schools in Scotland or England. At a School of this type, near my old College at Dundee, where one of these school buildings had been accidentally destroyed by fire, and was being again renewed by the boys, the admirable head-master said to me "It would pay the community though this happened every year! So extraordinary is the effect of this work upon our boys, not simply in manual skill, but in growth of intelligence as shown by school work all round. And above all in character!" Since then the war record of this school has vividly borne out this appreciation.

Of course such constructiveness is all but incredible to parents, teachers, and administrators of the old school; as with their own hearts chilled, hands useless, and thus heads dulled, by their past instruction, it cannot but be. The point here is, that experience is everywhere proving such efficiency; so that such criticism is negligible as argument, however disastrous as delay. I am old enough to remember when not only in England, but in India also, it was currently supposed that "Indians will never take to European Games!" Yet soon Indians were often beating Europeans at them. Why not next also for educational constructiveness in all its forms?

From such developed Boy Scout activities, already beginning in India, and surely soon to be developed in Patiala, let us pass to the highest developments of Indian Education, even beyond the University level, as the Universities will themselves admit—*e.g.*, the fertile research and teaching of Sir Jagadis Bose at Calcutta and Darjeeling, and the corresponding literary and cultural, spiritual and moral educative leadership of Dr. Rabindra Nath Tagore at Bolpur. Bose's great Research Institutes are after all but developments of his scientific workshop, not so long ago a quite small affair, which any good school would also soon improve on; while Bose himself, though peer of Kelvin, Marconi, and other leaders of Western Science, and indeed surpassing them in various ways, is able to do this because, like them, not simply "a man of genius" (*i.e.*, of high faculties freely developed throughout a strenuous life); but, like each of these, is a man of his hands; a mistri—developed as super-mistri, by fullest scientific effort of workmanship, surmounting all practical difficulties accordingly. And his students, among whom are not a few leaders of future science and education for India, are similarly effective; with hearts in their work and their hands skilful and resourceful; heads clear and original accordingly. They never think of cram; but "know their subject" by living the same life as their master.

Pass now to Shantineketan (Bolpur). There Tagore's School has long been growing; and its main feature is a good and varied library, in which the boys are free. I too, at Bombay University have also a new good and varied library, in which the students are free. But the difference is, that Tagore's boys read for themselves; since not sickened by drill and cram and exam over books which are not books, but only "text-books", mostly dry dung-cakes of the educational publishers. Whereas my students, though graduates to a man, and often of distinction—have gone through so many years of these prescribed drudgeries, that the very idea of free and wide and voracious reading over their subject and its associated fields, is strange and new to them. Too many never take to it; but those who do rightly call it "Convalescence". Then again I am a "Research Professor", but often beginning with students too late; their original thinking power—after all, personal common sense—having been crammed out of them, sometimes past recovery. But Tagore's boys have each the old habit of morning meditation, like their poet-master; and so their minds are researching already, though they may not know the word.

At Bolpur notably, the main teaching of every class, save in actual rain or wind-storm, is under the trees. In Bose and Tagore we have indeed essentially but reviving examples of the old thinker and educator sages of India, and each with pupils worthy of them, sitting together as of old; each group under its tree.

Enough them by way of justification of this plea for simple and economic planning; with ample ground, yet gradual growth of buildings.

Situation Recommended.

The large site suggested after discussion with leading educationists is therefore on plan shown north of road through Raghomajra, and west of the main Parkway. If the whole cannot at present be obtained, a delayed agreement might be arranged. But it is highly desirable to secure ample room for the workshop and the gardens of the future, as also for hostels for country boys, and for Teachers' houses.

Needed Playing Field.

Almost the only available place within the city ring, as already pointed out, available for a Playing-Field is that afforded by the fine little Park of Tobah Raghomajra. But as this is at present occupied as Police Drill ground, may I ask whether this may not be removed to an open field, south of Samadhan? On north side of road on plan. This is positively a little nearer to the Samania Gate Police Lines, and to Serai Magiki, and only a little further from Samania Gate and Barudkhana.

Conclusion.

In conclusion then it cannot be too clearly urged that the proposed location of this new High School so near the College is of mutual advantage. Now that education has been recognised by the University and admitted as a B. A. Course, this college is naturally called on to establish a Training Branch; and this requires a School within easy distance where its students, with least possible interruption of college hours by journeys to and from, can learn the practice of teaching.

The situation recommended, and indicated on plan, more fully meets these (and all other above) conditions than any other in the city.

CHAPTER XVII.

Further Areas for Planning.

Demand, and where to meet it ?

The proposed allotment of the Old Jail Area and neighbourhood to new housing, etc., (Chap. XI) utilises the most obvious vacant site of the whole city ; but it is necessary to find others to meet future demands. In what direction can we look ?

The natural direction of expansion of all cities of the Northern hemisphere, when possible, is predominantly westwards, or S. W., (largely since people naturally like to live windward, and also to move towards the sunset after the day's work, and again towards the light in the morning). The long line of Tobahs and their connecting Drain Nala, have in the past substantially checked this westward extension for Patiala, and even though this line be now made an attractive Parkway, the northerly available sites are already occupied by a very few spacious compounds around large mansions, which are not likely to give off much space, if any.

The large Haveli Kanwarji Sahib, now the Law Courts, may possibly yield space in its ample and well planted grounds, for three or four official residences, as for Judges. These Law Courts, however, also suggest one of the main sources of demand for new houses in every capital city, that of the many and prosperous lawyers ; and their need of sites may possibly be evoked, and met, to some extent, upon the fringes of the large Kothis to north and south, sometimes next the west Canal Boulevard, or towards the City as may be arranged. In seeking sites we thus come to south of the Tehsil, where there is but a little space available.

Philkhana.

South of Samania Gate Road however, we have the large enclosure of Philkhana. From this area we have already proposed to remove the elephants to the Zoo (Chap. VI), and the cattle also, to the same neighbourhood. If this recommendation be accepted, this large area can now be replanned, and so as to retain and utilise most of the existing buildings, as out-houses, for servants, &c., so that the change should work out with some profit to the State, as well as extension to the Housing Area of the City.

Topkhana and Beyond—New Garden Suburb.

Now Topkhana. This long-established situation for the Artillery is surely superseded by the removal of all other Military Forces to their well arranged and well built accommodation outside the city to

W. and N. W.? So it may now be proposed that the Artillery should also be removed from this old and now isolated position to take up its natural situation beside these. Military training and organisation would thus be more unified than at present; and the expense of the change should be fully met by disposing of the large area of land set free. For this is not merely the Topkhana itself, but the large open area behind it westwards to the Canal, and from Samania Gate (or rather Police Division No. 2) most of the way to the Raghomajra Road.

It is not forgotten that the State Carriages are also lodged in Topkhana; but these occupy but a moderate proportion of its space and need not at present be disturbed, or at most concentrated a little.

We have thus here—if and when the area can become available—the one remaining large possible space in Patiala for a new suburb. Its Planning is adjusted, so as to yield a fair number of holdings, varied in size to suit purchasers; while the main crossing avenues and central features are laid out so as to give unity and dignity to the scheme, and with formal regularity. This will be pleasing, in contrast alike to the sinuous variety of the Parkway, and to the general irregularity of the city's old streets, which can seldom be widened, and hardly anywhere straightened, without unduly large and unprofitable expense, which cannot therefore be recommended.

Area South of Topkhana.

The area between this above considered and the Raghomajra Road is too irregularly occupied, with houses of various value and character, to admit of re-planning. Enough here to utilise remaining sites as required, and keep the municipal standards of breadths for roads and lanes from being encroached upon, and made too narrow.

This quarter,—and also that of the larger Raghomajra south of the main road towards Qila—clearly illustrate the westerly expansion above referred to, which has been checked elsewhere. The outer half of this Mohalla has been regularly planned; and, though in lanes rather than streets, it is in fair condition, pretty free from dilapidation. On the inner and townward side, the old Mohalla irregularity may readily yield some open space for play and shade. Beyond this the proposed extension of the College leaves no available building space. Inside Samania Gate and opposite the Police Lines, some small houses have fallen away. Their site may be suitable for larger pukka ones.

Raghomajra Road and View towards Qila.

If the new High School comes to be located to N. W. of this road as already suggested, the adjacent side of the road may yield sites for buildings, as of houses for its lower and even higher staff.

Coming now to the crossing of Topkhana Road, it is well to point out that here—as the accompanying sketch clearly shows—we have the best view of the Qila which can now be seen from any road of the city. Yet this too is a good deal obscured by several small one-storey houses on the S. E. side, and if even one of these be raised a storey, this view will be spoiled. Here there is a strong argument for their removal, as not an expensive matter; and there is space for their replacement in the almost vacant angle between the two roads, without any serious separation of these cultivators from their ground.

With this small clearance, we have a fine architectural landscape, of the old city gathered around the fine castellated skyline of this great old Palace. New houses may be erected on the opposite side (northward) side of the road, commanding this fine prospect without injuring it.

Raghomajra Road continued to Qila (S. W. Angle.)

Leaving behind us the Tobahs, large and small, the district on the left hand between this road and the parallel one from Topkhana, and containing the small Tobah Gian Singh, shou d have this also improved as the local open space and Playground, and with a few shade trees and flowering trees for attractiveness.

Old Raghomajra.

On the right hand is the large mass of old Raghomajra. Too closely built though it is, and with lanes encroached on till too narrow, these do not admit of widening, or even of interconnection, without undue expense. Fortunately this Mohalla stands fairly high above the Park, and its lanes give access to this. The proposed new path, with seats along the bank sloping down to the Park, will attract people; and if a Garden, (say that beside the Telegraph Office) can be obtained, planted, and reserved as a Zenana Garden, it will yield its crop in improved health for this neighbourhood.

Further Possible Garden Suburb (on Baraderi Rajbaha, near College).

Though the present Main Boulevard of Patiala—as we must call the Baraderi Rajbaha—has begun well, next its Baraderi end, with the handsome buildings of the Singh Sabha and the Masonic Hall, it does not present many sites for further development. First a few private Bungalows follow these; then the Polo Ground, and next H. H. the Maharaja's Kothi. But the fairly large triangular area at first suggested for the Zoological Garden, on the opposite side from the College, and bounded on the northward by the Raghomajra Road, and of (say) sixteen acres in extent, affords a very suitable area for laying out as a small Garden Suburb—and its convenient accesses in all directions are greatly in its favour. Alternative plans are therefore drafted accordingly: and in such way that two or more of the suggested plots may readily be thrown together, for larger grounds and bungalows, as may be desired. That figured in City plan herewith is for smaller scale of holdings.

Proposed Sikh Hostel.

Returning to the Singh Sabha, a sketch plan has been prepared for the proposed Sikh Hostel, for School boys, College students, and young men employed in city, upon the vacant field to southwards; and is shown on general City plan accordingly.

CHAPTER XVIII.

Central Bazar Quarter and its Improvement.

Main Bazar area—Proposed Extension.

Returning to the main road, and reaching the NW angle of the Qila, we are fairly entering the Business Quarter of the City. But how marked the contrast between this side of the Water Tank area, and the other so much more active! How can this point be improved for business purposes? And at the same time cannot the congestion be lessened at the turn round the Tank, where Bazar Adaulat comes straight towards it?

Both results can be reached, inexpensively and profitably, by continuing this straight road from Raghomajra directly into the Bazar Shah Nashin. By cutting away the back of the Tank Garden, parallel to the Palace wall, room can be left for a row of shops against the wall; a fair number, at the present average Bazar breadth of 12 feet and depth of 20 feet. Next, allowing beyond these a 16 feet roadway (for Bazars pay best when narrow) or say 18 feet at most, we have still room for an opposite row of 18 or 20 feet deep shops with their backs towards the Tank. These are new shops added to the Palace Bazar series and its State rental; from which total however we have now to deduct the two shops which will have to be cut away at the curve of the existing Bazar, making therefore a very useful and profitable extension of the busy bazar Shah Nashin. So here is a case of an improvement which will help to pay for others. See Plan.

The Tank has still a space between it and the back of the shops; and the present iron gateway from the Palace into the Tank garden seems quite disused. In plan it is shown built up, by a shop covering it; but the passage can be left; or if later needed, the shop can be removed.

This Bazar Enlargement has the double value of extending and improving the present active Bazar Area, and of tending to develop the present backward one, upon the side by which we have come into town. There seems reason to expect fairly rapid increase of activity and value on this side. And in time, if further demand for shops at this angle of the Qila should develop, these can be obtained on the present site of the Vegetable Market (Subzi Mandi), pushing it upon the next vacant space behind the Qila.

Adjacent Temple Improvement.

Turning now from Bazar Shah Nashin towards Bazar Adalat, the beautiful little temple at the junction of the roads is at present practically smothered by very small shops which also encroach upon the road. These should partly be set back, partly removed, as shown on plan. Those set back may suffer in custom by less conspicuousness; but this will be partly compensated by cutting through the wall at the N. E. course of the temple enclosure, so as to open the adjacent lane, at present ending against this wall, with new entrance (for foot passengers, not vehicles) accordingly to and from the neighbouring quarter, and fresh customers also. The accompanying pair of water-colour sketches clearly illustrate present aspect, and easy improvement, respectively.

Samania Gate Road to Qila (S. E. Angle).

This road is fairly satisfactory as a thoroughfare in its outward portion, and as far as Telegraph Office and Samadhan, where the improvement of the Square has also to be suggested (page 82). But beyond this, dilapidation increases, upto the crossing of the long thoroughfare of Palangawala Bazar—(and its continuance at first as Seed Bazar, and then as Bamboo Bazar, and thus as main street of old Raghomajra to Subzi Mandi and neighbourhood, whose improvement has been above proposed).

At this crossing, the shops are close together, but are obviously of much inferior value to those of the Palace Bazar area, though this comes down parallel to the whole south of the Qila, by Katra Naourian, a wide and busy street, in fact the most satisfactory of the whole Bazar Quarter.

Needed Road Junction Improvement: New Square.

This sudden contrast in business and property values, and in aspect accordingly, seems largely to be explained by the too irregular and twisted turnings of the main thoroughfare, and with unsightly result accordingly. Here therefore is a road-junction needing a thorough-going improvement, and I trust rewarding it before long in business values, as certainly from the first as regard communications and aspect. The Plan shows the formation of a Square (1) by cutting away the small shops on the left (N. W.) as far as the small Temple, (*b*) by improving, if not rebuilding, the opposite side. Further on (*c*) the road is again widened on the left by setting back the shop at present projecting. Also (*d*) the shop opposite this widened road at the angle of Misry Bazar, is also set back.

This deteriorated area can thus be transformed into a good and seemly one ; and with that favourable reaction upon the neighbouring streets which a Square of junction for them tends to give. The shops dispossessed cannot of course all be accommodated on the same area, but those erected may readily be found accommodation in the immediate neighbourhood and on the N. E. end of Samania Road.

Quarter S. E. of Misri Bazar.

Though this is a good straight street with convenient accesses, all beyond it to south and south-east to the very edge of the town, all the way between Serai Maijiki and Chawalmandi as it runs out to Sanouri Gate, form a labyrinth, a sort of maze, a kind of traffic trap, which is more difficult to get through, or get out of, than any other area in Patiala. It may be said at first impression that the district is not one of great value, and thus will not reward expenditure or improvement. But this is too limited a view. It has suffered greatly in value, from the confusion of its streets and lanes, and is depreciated accordingly. But by cutting some connections, of course specially through Kholas where possible, and other points through inferior property, this whole area can be substantially appreciated in value, as it gains in accessibility.

That this has been realised by the Municipal Council is manifest from the recent partial clearance and widing from the Palangawala Bazar, but a good deal more needs to be done, at and between various points. These are shown on Plan, and thus hardly need detailed description. It will be seen that care has been taken to find the most open, and least expensive, line of alteration.

CHAPTER XIX.

Samadhan to Serai Maijiki, etc.

Planning West and East of Samadhan.

Returning now northward beyond the College, following the road beside Jacob's Outfall to the junction of the three brick Nalas into the main Drain, it is easy to plant all this broken land and local unsightliness with quick growing trees. Further, before turning, either to left towards the Samania Mandir and Bazar—or to right towards the Serai Maijiki, we see the possibility of planting a fairly straight Avenue alignment (uniting too with the "Zoo Road" on the other side of Jacob's Outfall) through ground at present covered with bricks and rubbish, to the side entrance of the Samadhan. From this new road is further suggested on plan another, curving round the corner of the Samadhan Garden, and running towards the N. W. corner of the Serai Maijiki. On these roads fairly large plots are suggested near the Samadhan, and smaller ones towards the east, but all for detached houses each with fair sized ground; so that here may arise a small but pleasing Garden Village, within more moderate distance of the business quarter round the Qila than it is elsewhere possible to find upon the City's Plan.

Samadhan: Neighbourhood, and Grounds.

As these improvements develop, the rubbish and confusion between the N. E. side of the Samadhan and the adjacent main street from Ghalori gate towards the Bazar quarter will naturally be closed up and planted, with further improvements to this Samadhan neighbourhood. The remaining fourth side with main entrance (Samadhan Square), will gain greatly by planting, say with cypresses, as shown on plan, and by removing the uninhabited and ruinous rooms on the east side of the small Hindu Temple (in front of Samadhan) which should also be coloured and washed.

The inner Entrance Court of Samadhan can easily be tidied and simply gardened, with a row of palms near the buildings of each side, and climbers on the wall on left hand (on entering), which has no arcade. Finally the internal garden is easily improved: while small palms or low flowering trees, in regular order, may be planted on all sides close to the walls.

The next colour washing of the ground-floor and main building should be in warmer tone. It is too white at present for the fine marble above, which will show far better when thus in contrast.

Serai Maijiki.

It will be remembered (see the paragraphs above) that the improvement of the area south of Samadhan has just been outlined; and that we have a good drive from the main Parkway from Moti Bagh and College, etc, past the Nala Junction and along to Serai Maijiki. It is urgently desirable that this building,—on the whole the finest in Patiala—be kept from falling into further disrepair; for though the courtyards are more or less fully occupied by the Police, it is on the stately front block and wings on each side that the whole architectural effect depends. What of their repair for Police Officers' quarters?

Adjacent Road Improvement, and of Neighbourhood; Boulevard to Sanouri Gate.

Past this building, and its open space in front, there is already a road fairly passable to vehicles, immediately on the outside of the town. Despite its poor condition, and the unpleasant smoke of neighbouring potters, several good houses have been recently erected, with open view eastwards. Further on, the road is uneven and narrowed; and thence widens, but passes an unsightly and evil smelling town-sweepers' depot a little before reaching Darshani Nala beside Sanouri Gate Road.

The proposal must therefore be pressed for the replacement of these insanitary and manure-wasting Depots by a more cleanly and profitable scheme (see page 44). And, later, for the removal of the potters also, whose burnings so seriously depreciate all surrounding property values at present. So if these two serious nuisances are removed, this unstidy Road can be made, at very moderate expense for its improvements, into one of the most attractive pieces of walk and drive around the whole city. In fact this is one of the most desirable improvements we have yet come to, since that which is most readily reached for fresh air and open view over the field by the very large population on the three principal sides of the Qila. By planting trees along the short new street opened into it on plan from the labyrinth between it and Qila, and next by moderate improvement along Chawal Mandi Nala Street, people will be attracted to this then pleasant and attractive promenade, though at present so repellent.

Continuation (Towards Safabadi Gate), for Postponement.

Though on plan it seems attractive, there are difficulties. First of more potters, who should also be removed, as means allow. But next a much greater expense for new road-construction, as also a less open result; in fact here the fruit-gardens adjacent would shut off any view. For these reasons this extension, though so far attractive as continuing the circuit of the town, may best be left to the future, and can be considered at leisure, in future years, when the more urgent improvements discussed in this Report have been dealt with.

CHAPTER XX.

Burning Grounds: and Temples.

Improvement of Hindu Burning Grounds. (Marghatan & Ghalori Gate).

Owing to the absence of any river for disposal of the ashes, the unsightly habit has arisen of simply dumping these all over the ground. The planting of sacred trees, Pipals etc. and of these in regular order, and with the earth slightly raised around the rows, will leave a furrow between in which the ashes can be deposited. If desired, this furrow can be bridged with a stone, so that the ashes will not blow about, but sink quietly into the ground with the rains, and thus invigorate the sacred trees.

The second Burning ground, outside Ghalori Gate, is similarly in need of improvement, The expense of planting etc., is not serious: and may readily became a work of goodwill.

Adjacent Temples.

After improvement of the main Burning Ground, a renewal of interest in the small Temples on the way thither, with planting of their neighbourhood will naturally arise. Indeed, in time the many Temples of this country-side, of which some are of monumental magnitude, will again be appreciated, and be kept in repair and beauty accordingly.

Is not the Sanatan Samaj in a position to head and guide such renewal of interest in the Hindu Community ?

Mohammedan Graveyards.

As regards these I have no suggestions to offer, beyond the planting of trees, which would greatly improve their at present somewhat desolate aspect.

Temples and their easy and expensive Improvement : four Examples.

This subject has been already raised in Chapter XIII, etc., but is of such great impulse to the City Improvement that it may here be returned to.

As examples of temples at present of little credit to the Hindu Community, yet with a little care and moderate outlay capable of being made so, I may especially call attention :—

(1) To the fine old Temple and Tank—yet these left much neglected—which stand near the Canal Boulevard, and on the large vacant

triangular space between the Marghatan Bridge and that opposite Safabadi Gate. Might not the cleansing and care of this Tank, etc. be made a work of piety and public spirit ?

(2) The small group of shrines, needing only a little repair, and plantings which end the perspective of the Darshani Nala Road from behind the Palace Chowk and as this is a street peculiarly easily improved into an attractive and direct way from the crowded City Centre to the open Boulevard here so easily arranged, (page 83) the improvement here pled for would help on others.

(3) The most extreme spoiling of a temple—previously a beautiful feature and land-mark, and easily recovered,—by smothering it in shops, is that where the Bazar Adaulat turns to the left of the Water Tank on the way to the Palace, as already mentioned (page 80). Sketches are herewith given of the present state on things, and of the original state of things, as so easily restored; while accommodation for the shop-keepers can be partly found on the square beside the Temple. A large increase in number of shops on the area can also be provided for by the proposed new short street through the present enclosed ground between the Palace and Water Tank; and this will more than meet immediate demand. (It may also afford some compensation to the Temple, if this can be fairly claimed). Behind this Temple it will be noted that the adjacent. Lane is opened, by cutting an opening in the Temple wall, an obvious public convenience since an appreciable short-cut.

(4) Another example, improvable with very slight outlay, much less than the preceding, is that of the little Temple on West Side of Bazar Dharampura; of which the fairly large garden-space can so easily be brought into order, beauty and flower around its Arna (Barna) tree, which is one of the most charming of all sacred trees, and deserves liberal planting accordingly, not merely occasional, but more like the cherry blossom so beloved in Japan. Might not the little garden be reserved for Pardah women and children, who will not go to the Tobahs near ?

(5) One final example, though many others might be mentioned, is of course the large Daviji Temple.

Daviji Temple.

A few very slight improvements will make the aspect of this on all sides more effective. Thus the uselessly high N. E. wall running up to Mall should be lowered to its former height, say of 32 feet at most, thus showing Garden and Temple to advantage. The Metal Water Tower to east can easily be surrounded with flowering trees, say the *Arna* (*Crataeva religiosa*), and this and other sacred trees—(Krishna's blue-flowered Kadam. Siva's Bael, etc.) planted at vacant points and borders of the Temple Grounds. The few willow saplings near angle of Hospital Tank may be increased in number and will soon give this a pleasing feature.

The patch of shrubbery opposite N. E. entrance of Ijlas-i-Khas may be reduced, so as to give view of Temple from this point The small side Temple a little further south may be shown to advantage by lowering wall, and thus making the doorway more of a feature.

The waste of water from the leakage of the Temple Tank may easily be transformed to useful irrigation of the Temple grounds, with more permanent verdure and flowers accordingly. The supply of Temple flowers will thus be increased, and with beauty to the whol surroundings. The existing paths may be laid with red ash, and a new path taken round the Temple Tank.

CHAPTER XXI.

Lahori Road: Serai and Uses, Possible Garage &c.

Decline of Lahori Road.

This street is apparently of more moderate date than any other important one in Patiala, and the largest, straightest and most regular of all. Why then on the whole least prosperous of any, the most dilapidated of all in fact, through large distances, with more ruins (Kholas) than surviving buildings on one side and the other?

Partly for the reason that the Indian Public do not anywhere take to these long and drearily regular roads, of the European organising fashion before the Town-Planning movement. Rightly enough, they stick to the old Bazar streets, of which the irregularity gave the variety of aspect to which they are accustomed; and they will continue to do so until we plan so as to preserve this interest, yet assure them convenience, &c., too, as I trust is attended to in this report.

Moreover this, at first sight well-drawn, road has far too little access to and from the rest of the city; and it is thus less valuable, for either business or for homes, than it will be if we can now improve these city communications.

Thirdly, why did these shop and house-rows, so regularly built on what was doubtless intended to be a sanitary pattern, fall so largely into ruins? Obviously, as their remains and survivors still show, from their thoroughly insanitary plan and construction! For behind the front shop, are two rooms, with only such air and light as enters from the front, and no sign of even ventilation to the back, much less of window, still less of courtyard. First wrong planning and construction; then deathtraps, with families vanished and all in ruins; the whole in fact, a compressed summary of too much of the would be sanitation and economics of the industrial age, and in more places than Patiala.

Possible Improvements.

How now to remedy this? Leaving the general question of Kholas and their treatment for the moment, it is plainly manifest that no mere reconstruction, or continuance of such planning as here, can for a moment be considered as fit for habitation, such as commonly tends to arise behind shops. It is necessary to assure them, notably, a thorough draught of air, and light also: hence since sure to be used as dwellings, a decent courtyard should now be supplied also. This should have been done at the first, but still happily may be in many cases, from the abundant vacant spaces behind. Yet not unfrequently this is now blocked, usually by a kacha House. In these cases the replanning must deal with both together—and in each individual case as best it can. Sometimes a kacha house or room may most cheaply give way: sometimes only the shop, and one room behind can be rebuilt. But this is not satisfactory; better leave a Khola vacant, and clear the space for a lane, a garden, or a tree.

Sometimes two (or even more) of these Kholas may be thrown together into a single larger site, suitable for a good house, when space behind can also be obtained. Sometimes too a workshop or a store may utilise one or more Kholas, and so on, as prosperity returns.

Herewith on plan are shown (1) the existing state of things along the large section of Lahori Road from Old Jail Road to the road turning westward to Tobah Mool Chand (already discussed, page 64) and (2) suggestions towards its treatment by supply of courtyards, when possible, and throwing together of Kholas.

Lahori Road Serai.

The very large old Serai on the east side of this plan is falling into ruin. May it not with advantage be taken up for industrial use? This is not incompatible with repair, and utilisation for dwellings, or even with retention of such portion as use may justify for such continued use as a Serai as may still survive.

Of Serais there seem more than necessary in Patiala, though their use may be greater in other seasons. Still there are few, and no other large buildings in Patiala so suitable for the Grain Mills and other industries which become complained of when placed in or among private houses; so that some such convenient, economic and industrial arrangements might here or there be made, for such little used Serais which can be acquired, and with more active use of the remaining ones.

I therefore indicate on this Lahori Road Plan such improvements as this Serai gives ample room for.

Silk Industry.

Another suggestion is that this Serai might be utilized, at least in part, for the Silk Industry, at present unsuitably located; and in quarters we shall see later as needed for more appropriate local use.

Future Garage Accommodation.

Nothing is more obvious, for any planning forecast such as the present, than that the recent and present growth of the Motor Industry generally is but the beginning of much larger developments. The provision of adequate Garage and Repair accommodation is however easier in this City, as indeed in Indian cities generally, through the utilisation of one (or part of more than one) of the numerous old Serais, which are no longer so much used as of old. Surviving, as they essentially do, from the pre-Railway Age, of Road-communications, one (or parts of large ones) may now readily be re-adapted to the Motor Age, that of Road-communications anew; and this with an economy, and even efficiency, exceeding what has usually been possible in the West: since large interior space is cheaply obtained, and their surrounding buildings are readily adopted for all purposes, from separate garages, for private vehicles, dwellings for chauffeurs, &c., to that storage of goods which will also increase with the opening future of motor-lorry transport upon the roads of districts.

And though the time is not yet ripe for this in Patiala, it may confidently suggested that before many years old Serais will thus increasingly appreciate in value; so that their future may reasonably invite consideration from the Municipality, or the Chamber of Commerce, when this arises; and not simply be left to individual enterprise, legitimate and pioneering though this be.

The abundance of Kholas, as in the neighbourhood of the Lahori Road Serai, also suggests additional facilities for replanning.

Lahori Road as Station Approach and City Entrance.

Such little life and prosperity as this Road and its adjacent quarter still possesses is to a large extent dependent upon its position, as a main Approach to the Railway Station, and a main City Entrance from it. Hence, although Railway Improvements and Developments have naturally to be settled upon their own merits: the interest (one may almost say survival) of this quarter is worthy of some compensatory consideration: since that removal of the Railway Station which is contemplated cannot but involve speedy and serious consequences to this quarter, as well as modification of others.

Existing Station Neighbourhood as Industrial Quarter.

The Development of this not inconsiderable area beyond the Railway and Station has been arrested by the extraordinary and persistent nuisance created by the Distillery. But this is entirely unnecessary; since by conducting it with ordinary technical competence and economy, this nuisance need no longer continue, but at once be brought to an end.

The advantage for industrial development of this area is not simply that of present convenience to Railway, but also to the City; and this again not merely by abatement of Cartage, etc., but by its convenient access for labour, from Patiala homes, without that need (and disadvantage) of capital outlay for Housing of workers, which necessarily must arise at any new industrial locations, beyond such moderate walking distance as that of this area. Nor is this simply a matter of convenience to workers, and economy to management. The experience of cities shows that industrial disputes arise much less frequently where the workers come from their homes throughout the city, than when they are lodged together, at the works, in "Lines" or "Chawls";—at best an unsatisfactory form of citizenship, and thus reacting unfavourably upon all concerned.

Finally, the rise of industries in this Station Quarter would tend to repopulate and renew this Lahori Road Quarter. Hence advantage and improvement of this portion of the City, and compensation for the removal of the Station, when that comes to pass.

Possible Timber and Fuel Yards.

The lower-lying area South of the Station might readily afford accommodation for Timber and Fuel yards, such as tend to be displaced by the present schemes of City Improvement, and which are at present often of a magnitude dangerous in case of fire. If sites here can be granted on easy terms, the town Fuel-yards can be reduced in dimensions; and with advantage to safety. Other Fuel-yards might similarly be granted on sites on important roads entering by various city Gates.

Possible Bonded Warehouse.

Though for this a city location is also being suggested (Chapter XXIII last para), this may afford a good situation, especially for bulky goods.

Possible Small Market.

In association with the development of the New Municipal Office (Old Jail) area, a small market is indicated on city Plan herewith, next Lahori Road: which may thus help improvement of both quarters.

CHAPTER XXII.

Kholas (Ruins) and their Possible Treatment.

Kholas of Patiala.

The extraordinary number of these kholas has been exercising me since my first visit, as far exceeding anything I have seen or heard of in other cities; (and is doubtless mainly explained by the fall of population through Plague, Malaria, etc. during several years, after the 1900 Census). The bad effect of these ruins, on public health, and in demoralising the sweepers by easy avoidance of labour, the Municipal file on this subject clearly recognises. Yet it hardly enough expresses the corresponding depreciation of the value of surrounding property; as well as the discouragement to the population, and to the city's credit and good name, which such tumble-down conditions produce, as also bad example to other towns of the State.

Utilisation of Rubbish.

Before entering upon larger questions, it may be asked—would not a good few of the proprietors be willing to bear a proportion of the cost of removing rubbish? It is only fair that the corporation should also pay good part (since its sweepers have so long been contributing). And would not same gladly sell now, and at very moderate valuation? Most proprietors, however, will not contribute to the expense and many no doubt cannot.

Diminishing cost of cartage, a large quantity can be used in almost every Tobah, and in various other open spaces besides, for the construction of slightly raised terraces or platforms (like that in front of the Arya Samaj building). These can be given a tidy surface, and should be planted with pipal, banyan, neem and other drought-resisting and shade-giving trees, which people enjoy, and learn to come and sit under. The edge of this platform or terrace needs support, for which old bricks abound in Patiala; and a good many would be yielded by the rubbish itself. The labour for this brick-work is not very expensive, but good mortar must be used, and cement at top. Some of these shade terraces are shown in plans.

Another use for this enormous quantity of rubbish, elsewhere indicated (Chapter VI) is suggested by its large amount of manurial matter, and also of lime, etc. for top-dressing of public pasture in the neighbourhood of the city, and before the rainy season (for which use the previous separation of the bricks etc. is easy). An increased yield of grass, and of milk accordingly, would result.

Need of Powers by Corporation.

Next the question of the *increased powers of dealing with these kholas*, which the Corporation has so long been asking (as per file and concluding letter from Home Minister).

There is no doubt that such powers are not given in the Punjab Municipal Act; and therefore they are not exercised by any of the towns referred to.

But here town-planning progress can help. In Britain the powers of cities were formerly as limited; and their kholas had to be endured. But the progress of legal thought had meantime been going on. The powers of a proprietor for "use and abuse", are increasingly being limited to "use and non-use"; while all abuses, and first those to public health, are being more and more strictly limited, by its advancing legislation and strongly dealt with.

Full Powers of British Corporations.

Secondly, the town-planning movement has encouraged British cities. Edinburgh took the lead, and first obtained, now a good many years ago, those very powers which this Municipality has been asking for—*viz*, that of summoning a proprietor, (1) to remove rubbish; (ii) to submit plans within three months, and begin repairs in not more than six months from date of notice duly delivered. When (as often at first happened) the proprietor of the ruinous building fails to obey this order; (iii) a second order is sent, with notice that if repairs are not satisfactorily begun, on plans duly approved by Municipal Council within six months more, (making twelve months in all), the property will be taken over by the Corporation and *sold by them at public auction.*—(iv) The buyer (which may be the Corporation itself) is bound to clear and demolish, repair or rebuild to the satisfaction of the Corporation, beginning within six months after the purchase. The title is then given with guarantee of the Corporation. Any subsequent dispute as to ownership is passed back to the original proprietor; who receives, however, the proceeds of the sale, less expenses).

No serious hardship has arisen from this, nor even discontent. On the contrary, public opinion strongly supports such improvement; and the proprietor is better off with small proceeds than with no return.

Improving Situation in India.

The reform of the Punjab Municipal Act on this and other matters connected with public health, town-planning etc. is thus only a question of time. As the Punjab Government becomes aroused to the progress of legislation in these matters in Britain, it will certainly follow, as other Indian Governments are doing. Moreover this State is under no obligation to await such tardy improvement; and it can surely readily take this useful initiative, from its own central authority, and with European sources of example in these matters. Madras, Bengal, Bombay and Central provinces have all been progressing in these matters.

Difficulties in Patiala.

Now, however, comes in the special difficulty in Patiala. There can be no purchasers for many of these kholas, so auction will fail as an effective measure. The Corporation should certainly obtain these powers: they will be effective in well chosen cases; but not in 821: so that extensive improvement cannot here be depended on, as in cities which have only a few kholas at a time.

Here, therefore, some larger remedy is needed: and this, I submit, can be found on the general Town Improvement scheme herewith submitted (in course of the few years needed for its development).

Improvement Trusts in India: Lucknow, etc.

In India it has generally been thought expedient to establish an "Improvement Trust," as at Bombay, Calcutta, Cawnpore and other cities. These, however, I am compelled to say—from repeated inspections and past Reports—are subject to grave dangers, as of promoting excessive demolitions; whence site speculations accordingly: and thus with great outlays, yet long continued scarcity of dwellings, and rise of rentals accordingly. Lucknow, however, is as yet singularly free of these errors; and before coming to Patiala at this time, I obtained the promise of the admirable Executive Officer of the Lucknow Improvement Trust (Mr. W. Botting) (i) to welcome any one sent from Patiala who may wish to look into these methods, and (ii) to give a short course of training, as one of his personal Assistants, to any officer who may be selected for that class of work in Patiala.

Possible modified method : Public Utility Society.

More modest, yet kindred methods, is that of forming a "Public Utility Society" to take up this work of Improvement—of course under the supervision of the Government, and of the Municipality, and including upon its board leading representatives of these, (to one of whom the Chairmanship would naturally fall). (For the purpose of concreteness, let me call this "Pukka Patiala" (say P. P. until the Government or Corporation give it a better name).

Suppose this group of active city improvers (P. P.) to be constituted under authority as above, how will it proceed ?

Suggested procedure and finance.

The first idea and desire would no doubt be (*a*) to obtain such grant from the State (whether by donation or by loan, at no interest, or at such reduced interest as may be arranged)—as would enable it to buy and repair kholas, etc., and do other work approved upon the Town-plan. It would also (*b*) ask the Municipality to contribute as far as possible. It might further (*c*) invite loans on deposit at moderate interest from public-spirited citizens interested in the improvement of the city (for such there are) ; and also (*d*) when its operation were advancing, it might obtain Bank advances. (But here the interest might be a difficulty, since the return from such property is below bank rate).

Such a Society would deal especially with remunerative property. But parts of every town-planning scheme of improvement—though tending to the enhancement of property values—are not of direct cash return. These improvements—as of street widening, park-making and improving, provision of open spaces, as play-grounds and *zenana gardens* (an immense advantage to women and children, who soon use them) can only pay indirectly : though in this way they pay well, as health returns soon show.

Distinct funds and accounts, etc., are thus needed for these two classes of operations. For both are needed, and the second class stimulates the first.

Further possible difficulty and methods.

Next suppose that at the present juncture—in the tightness of funds which all Governments (and Municipalities too) are more or less experiencing since the war—that no sufficient grants can be obtained by the new organisation ? It would thus have little prospect of deposits either : and would need cash badly. What can still be done ?

Suppose it to ask the State and Municipality to give—or at least deposit in its charge—their *lands and sites* within the city—*e.g.*, Old Jail Area, Tobah margins, and other vacant sites.

Next let it obtain powers to take charge of kholas, which the proprietors cannot themselves clear or repair, yet with due regard to their proprietorship. This might be done by crediting these with the amount of value (ascertained by arbitration if necessary) ; but of course paying no capital value, interest or rental, until rendered of cash value, and yielding a return.

The New Society (P. P.) thus becomes like the administrator of a deteriorated estate—with much land, but no money sufficient to improve this. (But given powers in its constitution, granted by the State) it might act like such an administrator ; and borrow some money to begin operations upon this large total security of land, sites and old buildings. If money can be borrowed from State or City, at low interest or none, so much the better : but even if interest has to be paid, a start can be made and an example given. For experience shows that even a general city depression such as that of Patiala in this matter can be overcome, and even speedily.

Thus, given the planning of such areas, (*e.g.*, Old Jail, etc.) into attractive holdings, demand can be created. In Indore we soon obtained over 700 applications for such holdings ; so that a more moderate but still sufficient number, to begin with, need not be despaired of in Patiala.

Cash payments, for such sites for new homes, will thus begin to come in ; in some cases by direct purchase ; in others by gradual purchase, spread over a term of years.

The New Society (P. P.) can also attract people towards building (or repairing, their kholas or elsewhere) by the advantages it can offer, of varied and suitable house plans, and of the economy afforded by larger contracts, *e.g.*, building half a dozen houses at once ; since the householder thus gets a better house, and more cheaply, than by dealing individually with a builder.

Finally, as the sites thus provided are taken up, the State and City should not ask for cash payment ; but should allow one-half (say) of the proceeds to remain in the capital of the Society, and the other half to be expended on such general improvements of the city as they may consider most conducive to the general interests of the community.

The advantage of the above arrangement is that it would enable a start to be made, without waiting for grants. Moreover it does not prevent subsequent applications to State and City for these, to carry out improvements, more extensively when finance is easier, and fuller interest is created by these useful beginnings.

CHAPTER XXIII.

Central Patiala.

General Features.

This Improvement Scheme has hitherto been steadily working its way from the circumference of the City inwards; and towards the old and historic City, which we have only now reached.

By thus proceeding along the lines of least resistance, it has been found possible—with much less of alteration and demolition than at first sight appeared probable, and thus at correspondingly moderate expense—to plan out a large number of separately moderate changes. But these, in aggregate, will be seen to yield many improved communications throughout the largest area of the City. In fact, as many as its moderate population requires; and as its also moderate finances can be expected to make, and to maintain, with advantage.

Recall the main features of this Scheme so far :—(1) the Park-way, from Moti Bagh and past College up to Ijlas-i-khas and Baradari; following (and improving the aspect of) the present Drainway, through Raghomajra and other old Tobahs; (2) the similar development along Central Nala, thus becoming practically a new and attractive Boulevard; with street improvement up to Tobah Mal Chand, and thence across Lahori Road to the Canal and Station Boulevard. We have thus crossed the City in both directions: (1) by the Park-way, following (and improving the aspect of) the present Drainway through Raghomajra and other old Tobabs. Furthermore, the two areas planned out for new dwellings with moderate sized gardens—viz (3) the old Jail Area, and north-wards to Hospital Tank etc, and (4) that of Phil-Khana etc. and the open space beyond, as far as the Canal and Baradari Rajbaha. These sites will tend to attract some of the present residents of the old City, and thus tend to check any further new building there—which can indeed now be prohibited, with advantage to public health etc. Repairs of course should be encouraged: but the ruinous houses in this Central Area of the City should be taken over, and removed, for open spaces and squares; thus improving property values, and also communications

Typical Narrow Streets: Improvement in Detail

Such needed open spaces can be obtained most cheaply by demolitions of ruinous houses in the overcrowded lanes of back lanes, or by acquisition of vacant sites and fuel-yards—(for which new accommodation is easily obtained at no great distance, as in the Tobah along the Central Nala, and in vacant areas towards Safabadi Gate).

Take however the case of Kacha Desraj and Kacha Bhandian. Here are good old houses, well worth keeping up; but depreciated because of their extreme narrowness, at too many points preventing the passage of vehicles in opposite directions, and thus practically deterring use as thoroughfares.

To a slight but useful extent widenings are necessary: and there are proposed as follows:—

(A) From the little square at the corner of the meeting of Bazar Nashin and Bazar Bazazan (N. E. Corner of Qila) moderate widenings are shown on plan herewith. These improve the access to both these streets; and especially the westward end of K. Bhandian The widening however ends so far as that street is concerned, at what is at present the front yard occupied by the Goala. But this space, easily acquired at moderate outlay, affords what is almost a small square, and thus a fairly wide turning for vehicles. Furthermore, from and through this area is shown on plan a proposed new thoroughfare northwards to meet the Central Nala, and near the middle of its course—at present practically inaccessible, save on foot, and through a long zigzag of lanes.

(B) These two streets are also narrowed throughout their course by the many projections of steps from the houses, which mostly encroach into the roadway. But these can be set back; and at only a very moderate expense, for each of the houses; and this outlay would be far more than compensated by their increased value, which would result by making these streets passable for vehicles. Three perspective sketches are therefore deposited with this Report, (1) showing the too common type of encroachment on the roadway: (2) the moderate setting back of this, by a foot or so, so as merely to cover the street gutter, (where this set-back is enough to give the necessary minimum breadth: and (3) the fuller setting-back which is necessary at points of extreme narrowness (This last may sometimes involve a step within the entrance of the house: no doubt at first a slight inconvenience, but less expensive than the lowering of the whole floor). Chabutras must of course also at times be cut back, where necessary for passage.

Finally (4) at one, two, and when possible three, points along each street, (as may be practicable with rebuilding), the frontage should be set back, sufficiently to afford a safe and easy "siding", where one vehicle can wait to let another pass it.

With these modest improvements, these two streets, in aggregate of a very considerable value, can at small expense be greatly appreciated.

Moreover, these methods can be gradually applied, as opportunities arise, throughout many (and ultimately all) of the many excessive narrowings of the streets, and often of the lanes of the City. No doubt at times Municipal pressure may need to be applied, and the expense of alteration may have to be contributed to, in the case of poorer owners: but on the whole, the appreciation of property-values will be increasingly seen by all concerned to justify these moderate widenings. For each person soon comes to see the advantage to his property by these slight settings-back of his neighbours; and he thus finds resistance more difficult when it comes to his own turn, and their opinion acts upon him.

Encroachments by Shopkeepers.

This has been and is, in Patiala, as everywhere in Indian Cities, a main source of narrowing. It is of course so far restrained by control: and with that development of such Municipal Improvement Committee, or other Authority, (as is usual after a Town Improvement Report), its Executive Officer will rapidly acquire not only fresh vigilance in preventing new encroachments, but also the needful experience, tact, and economy, in abating—or if need be removing—the worst cases of mischief already done by past encroachments.

Economies of "Conservative Surgery."

It is not in many occupations that one can boast that the longer one works, the less one seems to do: but as in surgery, so in town-improvement, the problem is to cut as moderately as possible; and here I recommend very little cutting indeed.

This city is not one which at present requires new wide thoroughfares: nor is it likely to require these within the generation now opening, even with that increase of motor circulation which is to be expected. Moreover, the scale of the town's buildings, corresponding to its very moderate wealth, gives no sufficient prospect of the larger and finer buildings which are required to give a good appearance to a wide and straight thoroughfare: nor does Bazar business anywhere profit by leaving its customary narrow streets, which are found far the best for shopping, as witness the Chowk of Lucknow, &c. &c.

Hence I have definitely had to abandon the idea which naturally occurred at first sight—that of widened and rebuilt Approaches to the Qila: though it will be seen that something has been done in that direction, as follows.

Improvements of Approaches to Qila.

First, that from Moti Bagh by Baraderi Rajbaha and Raghomajra Road, will be substantially improved and widened: (a) if the new High School site (Chap.) be approved, by setting-back the present (mostly kucha) buildings, and replacing these by Masters' Houses with gardens. The one fine distant view of the Qila possible in the City, and picturesquely seen above old Raghomajra, is shown in the accompanying water-colour sketch, near North West corner of Tobah Raghomajra. From that the road crosses the Drainway—now proposed Parkway—(and thus a practically renewed approach so far) and then runs on, (with setting-back of a few feet as rebuildings take place), to past Subzi Mandi to the Qila direct: *i. e.* going straight through the (short but profitable) proposed new extension of the Bazar Nashin, instead of passing round the Water Tank as at present.

Second, the existing way by the Samania Bazar is readily improved by the moderate Square there proposed, to replace the irregular crossing of this Road with the Plangawala Bazar, and the meeting with Misri Bazar (Chapter XVIII, and Plan). After this, the Katra Naourian is a good wide street, and the moderate extention of the Chauk Kasarian is also recommended (as on Plan) towards Chawal Mandi.

Third, the proposed External Boulevard, from Serai Maigiki towards Sanouri Gate, arises from the simple improvement of the present untidy road. The Darshani Nala also admits of that moderate widening: at narrow points: and with planting of a few trees—(and perhaps covering in this portion of the brick drain,— if floods allow this ?) it will make a quite respectable approach to the Palace Chouk.

Fourth, I have of course carefully considered the possibility of widening the present main approach to Qila from Baraderi and Ijlas-I-Khas; by Bazar Adalat, and have submitted suggestions (Chapter XIV) at various points *e. g.* Chouk Routan, and at Temple corner, opposite Water Tank especially.

Fifth, as supplementing this route, and to a moderate extent diverting traffic, there has also been proposed (Chapter XIII and Plan) an improved continuation from Bazar Sheranwala down to Nala Kashmirian, and as far as Central Nala. To continue this route to Qila, and as directly as may be, is of course a tempting project: but observation shows the intervention of irregular and expensive buildings. Yet, on this route, the formation of an intermediate Square is indicated on Plan, by opening out the irregular and partly open area of little value, south of the street behind Singh Sabha and Primary School:—and from this cuts are made, as inexpensively as is possible, and giving a fairly direct route, with resulting possible new buildings, and improved values in this at present poor quarter.

Sixth, the improvement of the Sirhandi Bazar and Safabadi Bazar route to and from Qila has also been much considered. But any substantial widening would be too expensive, though re-building should be set back. A small Square is however obtainable, by cutting back the south side of the obtuse angle at which these roads meet, and the Bazar Chatamagniram comes in from northward: and as this is the main point of congestion, this widening will be useful as well as seemly. Other slight widenings are also indicated on Plan.

Further Improvement of Aspect of these Qila Approaches.

So far, it has not proved possible to do anything impressive in the way of fine broad new thoroughfares or widening of old ones: in fact, the state and means of the City do not admit of it: and were I to recommend any of this, the financial, as well as other results, would be disappointing.

Still, as the accompanying watercolours and pencil sketches show, the Old Town does not lack elements of a quiet but varied local beauty; and by recovering the appreciation of these, and with continuance of detailed improvements such as these suggest, the whole city can again become seemly and pleasant. The study of the various paired watercolours, marked in each case A and B is therefore asked for: A giving the present untidy or squalid aspect, and B showing the improved aspect, easily obtained, as when an intervening ruin is removed, a tree or two planted, and so on. This line of simple improvement would soon work marvels throughout Patiala; and fill a photographic exhibition a few years hence.

The Whitewashing, which has produced so encouraging an effect from Sheranwala Gate to Qila, should also be encouraged throughout the town, and in these main Qila thoroughfares to begin with: hence Chapter VIII, as also the Tree-planting of "Arbor Day" (Chapter VII).

Improvement of Main Aspect of Qila by Chowk.

One improvement however is possible, with no great expense, and fine effect: viz, the gradual improvement of the frontages of the buildings of the Chowk—so as to give an aspect more worthy of what it really is the public Fore-Court of this fine old Palace. The untidy vehicle repairing work of the N. W. Corner should be removed to a more outlying quarter; say to one of the open spaces available along Safabadi Bazar. The present Gate Archway to and from Sirhandi Bazar can be at little expense turreted and adorned. The outer improvement of the Gateway, the sky lines, and the colouring of the large Kotewali of the north side would readily give this a fuller harmony with the Palace. On the opposite side the buildings of the State Bank etc, will also give a good effect with moderate improvement. Even with better colouring all round these three sides of the Chowk, and also—at the next whitewashing of the Palace—the picking out of its beautiful ornamental detail, more or less as has been done inside, will give this whole Palace Chowk the fine Central effect for which it was designed from the first.

Possible Chamber of Commerce Building.

In this connection may also be mentioned the desirable removal of the Silk Department to more commodious and suitable Premises, (Chapter XXI) and the possible utilisation of that building for the conveniently central location of the Chamber of Commerce, which might so well advance the Business interests of the City, as in so many cities elsewhere.

Remaining New Thoroughfare from Qila to Proposed New Municipal Office.

The weak point so far, in my proposal of the utilisation and extension of the old Jail Building, as the future new Municipal Office, has of course been the want of direct communication between this and Qila. But this is also the worst feature of the whole City—its lack of a central thoroughfare in this direction. And though this has engaged me from the first, it has waited to the last for Air Photos, in absence of adequate City plan: and as these have not come to hand, my solution may need to be slightly modified on survey before execution.

It will however now be seen, on the approximate plan so far possible, that the new thoroughfare above referred to, from N. E. angle of Qila (meeting between Bazar Nashin and Janagali) runs up to Central Nala, while the corresponding new thoroughfare from new Municipal Office area (Old Jail) to Central Nala comes down not far off. To cut a straight thoroughfare all the way would be too expensive, and out of keeping with the rest of the town, but the proposed route will be seen to be fairly straight after all. Moreover, from the present Jail Archway it will be remembered that the proposed new straight Boulevard, centered on the Hospital Tank and Statue, runs northward. This combination and contrast will be pleasing:—that of the straight Boulevard, where inexpensively practicable, and through a substantially new quarter, planned to suit it—with the less regular new southward route, to Central Nala and thence to Qila, through old quarters which cannot now be regularly planned and rebuilt, without undue sacrifice, and practically prohibitive expense.

CHAPTER XXIV.

Further Developments of Agricultural and Technical Industries in Patiala.

Acknowledgments.

Towards the difficult task of writing this final chapter as to Patiala, I have not simply used my own observation and experience of the City, but have had the benefit of repeated discussion with the various official experts concerned. And particularly with Dr. Chakravarti for Chemical Industries, Sardar Harchand Singh for Agriculture and Horticulture, Sardar Wazir Chand for Silk-Industry, Sardar Nihal Singh for Forestry, and Sardar Ranbir Singh for Co-operative Societies, actual and possible. Hence to each and all of these gentlemen, as to others, my hearty thanks are due, and tendered.

Agricultural Suggestions.

My suggestions as to Forestry, to local Agricultural and Horticultural Developments, and Silk among these, are already given above (Chaps. VII, XXI etc.) : but the more general and also Chemical developments which appear to me as most practicable may now be summarised.

Thus without going into larger questions of Agriculture, I may plead that the suggested development of Agriculture in connection with the College, and its future necessary small Experimental Farm beyond the proposed Botanic Garden, may become of substantial service, just as with Agricultural education elsewhere. And further, that specific improvements, such as the utilisation for a Grass-meadow below the main Drain outlet, and the proposed top-dressing of the City's Pasture-fields with (sifted) Patiala rubbish, from Kholas etc. at the beginning of next rainy season, will be found of advantage, and suggestiveness elsewhere. With this fodder-development, goes also the production of Ensilage, still far too little made, used, or even known, in the Punjab.

Vegetables and Fruit: Pharmacy.

Similarly the Pinjaur Garden, (no less than the Patiala Botanic Garden and Experimental Farm, as they develop) may become a fertile centre. Thus for the improvement of Vegetables and Fruits—Mangos, Guavas, (and the drying of all these)—also the growth of Mulberry trees; and not only for Silk, but for pruning for fodder. Also the growing of Medicinal Plants, for which there is a constant and substantial demand, may readily lead to the development of productive industries of Pharmacy, as with the successful initiative of Prof. Sir J. B. Ray, near Calcutta. The extraction of alkaloids, medicinal or fragrant oils, etc. from such plants is there in remunerative progress. In this connection, it is of interest that the roses of Pinjaur in former years used to yield as much as a maund of flowers per day for distillation of Attar of Rose.

From this precious luxury to the preparation of medical remedies, and of dyes,—as also to the distillation or expression of more homely oils,—presents little difficulty to the industrial Chemist. Nor even the further working up of these oils, as for soap, for lubricants, etc., and with residual waste to cattle foods, or to manure.

Manure-Possibilities.

The scarcity of manure is one of the main limitations of Indian Agriculture, and not least so in the Punjab, or in Patiala. And though this can be to a substantial extent mitigated—as a wise Forestry-policy provides cheap fuel, and thus saves the present disastrous burning of cow-dung, with land-starving accordingly—there will still remain much need for other manures. Thus notably as regards phosphates. Nothing is more regretable to the rural eye than the current waste of bones. It is surprising that there is as yet no Bone-crushing Mill in the whole Punjab. Here there is a real opportunity, and for each of the two favourably situated railway towns of this State, Bhatinda and Rajpura, with their wide accessibility, alike for collection of the material, and for despatch of the results, throughout the State and beyond. The surviving prejudice against the use of bones will not last much longer.

The existing Nitre-Industry may similarly with advantage be associated with this. The preparation of various compound chemical manures can thus be aided, and with due adaptation to the requirements of particular soils, in which the modern chemist is skilled. The Nitre-Industry thus provides him with the raw material for nitric acid and nitrates generally.

Arts of Distillation.

His arts of distillation have also further applications, as notably in the distillation of wood and its waste, in connection with the Forestry Department; as also in the preparation of rosin and turpentine. Also Matches. Given rosin, printer's ink is easily produced, for which the demand is steady.

Again also in the distillation of industrial Alcohol, and even of local spirit. Thus the present nuisance, and amazing waste, of the Patiala Distillery can at once be removed, and with substantial economy and profit, alike to its immediate business return, and to its taxation accordingly. It needs but the application of that ordinary skill, care, and cleanliness, which has elsewhere become universal in distilleries throughout the World, since their reformation, nearly two generations ago, by their simple applications of the discoveries of Pasteur.

Glass-Industries.

The development of the Glass-Industries in its many forms offers hope; not simply on account of vast demand and high price throughout India, but also because of the excellent material which I am assured is obtainable in the State.

Use of Mica.

In this connection, let me also point out that the utilisation of the abundant, and relatively cheap, Mica of India, as a substitute for window-glass, is a practicable industry, and one which might afford an excellent outlet for the skill and taste of the Indian workman. Thus, were I building a house in India, I should use Mica. (as I have long ago experimentally done in my own home in Edinburgh), for small windows especially. Instead of the ordinary window-framing for glass-panes, it is easy to make and to use the leaden frame-strips of the glass-stainer; and thus to arrange Mica sheets of all shapes, sizes, and varieties of tint, with results of beauty—in their way as remarkable as those of lightly stained glass, and of course here at a fraction of its expense. Where the clear view of glass through an ordinary window is desired, this also can easily be arranged; by fixing an ordinary glass-pane at the eye-level, and thus within the more varied Mica-bordering.

Pottery, and Possible Developments.

Coming now to the Potter's art, so much in evidence in Patiala, there is scope for further developments. These might be readily provided for, on a moderate scale, in course of the removal of the College Potters' Village, and later of the others from the City. Thus that progress of horticulture, which cannot fail to take place as the Garden-City scheme of previous chapters is developed, may reasonably create a demand for flower-pots, for gardens and for balconies. And when an enterprising flower-gardener sends round through any town a barrow of pot-plants, he seldom fails to dispose of them, and profitably too.

But beyond these and other homely pots, why not also pots of beauty? Is it not possible to import a potter or two from Sind, with their traditional skill and taste, to inoculate some of the Patiala potters with the ambition of learning from them, even rivalling them, in the production of their magnificent blue-glaze pottery, with its not only Indian, but world-wide reputation? Thus for instance, the Flower-

Vases, which no doubt once adorned the main points of the central water-channel of the Pinjaur Garden, might be renewed, and more beautifully than ever: while their further application—as in gardens more generally, as well as in homes, and even for permanent external decoration of street-buildings—might also readily arise.

With this glazed pottery, goes also the making of glazed Tiles. I have lately seen the revival of this magnificent oriental industry in Jerusalem, and with its old-world beauty. Yet with a moderation of price which is admitting of the usual domestic uses, not only sanitary, but decorative. And also of public applications, as to the repair of the famous Dome of the Rock (the so-called Mosque of Omar), and even to that naming of the streets and lanes of the City, which is now in progress.

Wood Industries.

Return here to further developments of the Wood Industries. In connection with the very desirable repair of dwellings, there is need of good Timber, for rafters, flooring, door and window-frames, etc. With this the building of improved Hand-looms. Similarly of course for finer carpentry and Carving, up to those often marvellous and exquisite house-doors, which are still common throughout Old Patiala, and give such distinction to the homes within.

With this too should go a fresh impulse to Furniture-making and Cabinet-making. And these readily beyond home consumption; since outlets as far away as Lahore and Simla are not prohibitively distant. Carving is here again worth encouragement.

Mechanical and Electrical Industries.

The Motor industry, as already urged, has here a substantial future. Similarly, the increasing and cheapened supply of Electricity—which may reasonably be expected before many years, as the colossal water-power resources of the hills are brought under control—will admit of small motors, for all manner of industries.

Cotton Factories?

Coming now to the great Factory-Industry, is there any reason why to the Ginning of Cotton,—for which there are only too many factories in many Indian Cities, even if not yet in the Punjab, or in Patiala—there should not soon be added Spinning and Weaving Factories also? Indore shows very successful examples of these, as doubtless nearer cities. Of course the great distance and costly freight from Bombay give notable advantage to Punjab industry for its own productions. But the right situation? Not Patiala nor Bathinda—perhaps some less dry situaation.

Arts of Costume.

With cotton may be considered also all the other arts of Costume. Whatever respect be due to the recent ascetic advocacy of Khaddar home-spun, it may confidently be assumed that human nature will continue to desire materials and garments in which beauty is more provided for. The ladies of India, it is to be hoped, will never abandon their beautiful Saris; and even the men will not permanently endure our ugly and unsuitable western fashions, so deficient in beauty of form and colour alike. It needs to be realised by Indians that these "Western Fashions" are only nineteenth century adaptations to the atmosphere of its industrial age, so full of dust and smoke, and also to that total eclipse of the Arts which came in with its would-be utilitarian philosophy, now seen as futilitarian. Before that period, the male Western Costume was good in form ; and often as rich in colour, and even embroidery, as that of ladies: and so, with the passing of that modern mythology, (now more rapidly than Eastern Critics of "Western materialism" as yet recognise) there is no reason why the Indian gentleman should not abandon our ugly hats, jackets and dwarf elephant-legs, and return to the healthier and more picturesque costumes of his immediate predecessors. The turban—the most dignified and the most individual of all the head-gear of the world—will thus recover its old variety and even splendour, with continued employment to the textile arts accordingly. Artistic weaving, dyeing, embroidery and gold-work will thus revive. This last-named industry, it is to be hoped, will not be allowed to die out in Patiala. And similarly for the Indian gold-smiths and silver-smiths.

Need of Technical and Vocational Education.

The military establishment of Patiala gives evidence of careful technical education of its own kind, with aid from external experts also. Yet this is not directly productive, but has necessarily to be maintained from the taxation of the productive industries. So why should not these also be encouraged, and developed in ways, reasonably similar in principle, although of course quite different in detail ?

Hence, along with the improvements and developments of the College already outlined, may there not also be included beginnings of a Department of Technology—such as is arising so largely in connection with Universities throughout the West, and even now under active discussion in Bombay ? The gentlemen whose help has been recognised at the outset of this chapter, are each and all suitable additions and reinforcements to such a College Staff : yet, without the large expense of creating new chairs and fully equipped departments, might not each give a short course annually, to the few students who would be at first available, without appreciable loss of time to his State duties; but with that encouragement and stimulus which is given by the interest of a few intelligent hearers.

From this beginnings however, a Technical Workshop, and an Industrial Laboratory, would naturally arise. These would soon prove their value, not only in training a few students, but by aiding or initiating one after another of the above-mentioned or other Industries, (and thus in finding occupation, even career, for their students). Thus there would before many years be proved, to the satisfaction of the State, and of capitalists and skilled workmen also, the advantage of a Technical Institute, corresponding broadly to those already in existence at

Baroda, Gwalior, Kashmir, Mysore, etc: and conducted by a section of the Education Department centered on that Technical—and Vocational—Education which is so needed to reduce the present over-pressure upon the clerical and literary occupations.

The supply of scientific and technical experts with College education, and also of young Mistris, to replace the too rapidly vanishing old ones, would readily be increased by such a Technical Institute, with its day and evening classes.

We also need the analogous practical corrective to the too purely literary and commercial instruction of the Schools, not only secondary but even primary. This is increasingly being provided in various countries. Thus in Ceylon, every primary School has its Garden, with excellent results towards general education of its scholars, as well as development of their rural interests and efficiency. The growing experience of the west, from Russia to France, to Britain, to America, shows that the old dislike of the farmer and peasant to Schools and their education—hitherto too easily regarded by town educators as "mere prejudice"—was founded upon a natural and proper objection to their de-ruralising influences: and these the school-garden largely helps to cure. With the School-Garden should also go a simple Workshop, with various work-benches, and a simple loom or two. At these the youngsters soon learn the various makings and mendings in which their hands delight, and with far better results, even in ordinary lessons. Vocational aptitudes are thus discovered in good time, without the present delay, waste and misemployment for which the common type of Schools have so long prepared.

With this Garden and Workshop as parts of the school-life, Boy Scouting will fully improve its activities. For these are becoming as much the great game of this rising generation as were the ball-games of ours; and with far fuller educational result. Thus a new generation, of higher average efficiency than has been ours, is already coming in to manly activity: and from this a higher preparation of real distinction is thus being ensured.

Conclusions. Towards the close of a Report necessarily mainly devoted to the improvement of surroundings, buildings etc, it cannot now be too emphatically pressed that the development and improvement of a City, a Region, or a State, proceeds essentially with those of its People, and thus of the Rising Generation though to help this as it needs, we must also be re-invigorating ourselves, in spirit, in mind and body. Where is the best land in any site or locality? The true answer is not merely that of the geologist and chemist: "It is where you find the best farmers". And so for all the highest Occupations, Arts and Sciences: the natural and local advantages are but small in comparison with the quality of their men. And this quality is capable of indefinite improvement; for education is now emerging from its recent and too long surviving maze, of past errors—as of mechanical copy, cram, and verbiage, so long enforced by a well-meaning, but itself miseducated, bureaucracy.

Wealth and Welfare in the Punjab.

Finally, in this whole connection of Agricultural and Industrial Development, I must refer to a recent book—"Wealth and Welfare of the Punjab",—by Mr. H. Calvert, I. C. S., Registrar of Co-operative Societies, Lahore. (Rs. 6). Of the value of this to all interested in these questions—(as who is not?)—I cannot speak too highly, but may here refer to my reviews of it in the Bombay Co-operative Journal, and in the (London) Sociological Review:—of course, above all, to the book itself; which will be found of real service towards the clearing up of its reader's ideas, and on agricultural and urban developments and view-points alike.

LIST OF DRAWINGS AND SKETCHES DEPOSITED WITH PLANS OF PATIALA CITY

I. *Larger Drawings* :—

(1A) *Kutra Desraj Street* (S. W. end, in present state). Derelict Khola, almost hiding handsome temple, and congesting traffic.

(1B) The same, after proposed removal of Khola, forming an open square in front of temple.

(2A) *Mandir of Pala* seen from in front of Water tank near Qila—present state. The temple partly concealed by nearer shops.

(2B) The same; showing proposed improvement by removal of one or more shops, and planting of a sacred tree.

(5) Three drawings of a typical doorway on narrow street:—

(*a*) Steps projecting and encroaching on Street.

(*b*) Steps set back by cutting away wooden door-sill.

(*c*) The same; chabutra also cut away.

(4) *Temple Biramjir* (South end of Lahori Bazar near Safabadi gate). Walls shown lowered to former height, and fallen turret rebuilt.

(5) *View in Central Nala Parkway*, looking W; showing irregular and picturesque avenue treatment produced (*a*) by planting cypresses etc. where possible, (*b*) by wreathing existing railing with creepers, stretched at short intervals across brick Nala.

(6) *View near Arya Samaj building*, Tobah Mul Chand. Note picturesque grouping of temples.

(7) *House of Sardar Dhan Singh*, Mohalla Marasian; (behind mandir of Pala). Example of fine old houses, well worth conservation and repair.

(8) *Houses in Mohalla Fakeran,* Kutra Sahib Singh St. Compare No. 7.

(9) *Qila from Tobah Raghomajra.* The best general view of Qila—hence worth preserving.

II. Small Sketches:

1. (*a*) Ruin on Darshni Nala road (near Chouk Madar.)

   (*b*) Ruin cleared to reveal existing temple, garden extended.

2. (*a*) Bazar Shah Nazin looking South.

   (*b*) Bazar extended, through vacant space behind Water-tank to Raghomajra road.

(3) Small Samadha on "Nala Parkway'.

(4) Three pencil drawings on Bazar Chata Magni Ram.

(5) A City Gate in Patiala; Cypresses planted.

(6) Small temple opposite Ijlas-I-Khas, showing wall lowered. (This might be done to many temples with great addition to the beauty of the city.)

(7) Samadhan; interior of entrance court, showing improvement by setting back railings and planting palms.

CHAPTER XXV.

Note on Sanour.

As I have twice visited this town, in evening, and at early morning, I may submit my impressions, and suggestions accordingly.

The roads—even the main street through the town—are in very bad condition, yet the extraordinary quantity of old bricks everywhere, gives material for the main mass of needed repair material close at hand, so as to render cartage hardly necessary. Things have got so bad that a small grant may be necessary; but still more is encouraging leadership. This could be given by the loan of a fairly skilled and experienced, yet junior, officer from the Roads Department, chosen also for his powers of interesting the community, as well as his own workers, in this urgently needed improvement.

I was shown over a good new house nearly finished at the highest point of the main street; and the evident interest of the neighbours, as well as the workmen, and the enthusiasm of the owner over his new home, and its conveniences, its decoration too, as also its fine view over the town and surrounding country, were as good an instance as could be desired of that "*house-pride*", which was not so long ago general in Indian towns, and which has only to be encouraged anew, (as I have pled for Patiala), to set agoing a new period of repair, improvement of old dwellings, and the desirable amount of new building as well.

Again the School is most fortunate in its handsome and spacious location in the Old Palace: and evidently conducted with some scientific as well as literary teaching. I venture to plead however that a certain area of garden be allotted to the school, which would soon be found of great educational value and practical impulse; if, as may reasonably be hoped, one of the teaching staff, or even a friendly outsider can be found to give the requisite leadership. In that case the whole of the garden ground and orchard might soon be undertaken by the scholars.

May not a Town Improvement Association be encouraged with advantage ?

Note on Bahadur Garh.

This magnificent old fortress and its fine Palace are in themselves enough to attract visitors and tourists, and no one visiting Patiala City should miss their strikingly monumental contrast and combination. If Serai and Dak Bungalow accommodation be adequate, the little town would readily profit by increased custom; and Patiala people would also increasingly find a pleasant holiday outlet and change.

Note on Rajpura.

Here I have had no time for study: yet I cannot but think there are substantial opportunities for local improvement, and even for over agricultural and economic development, at so very favourable a railway situation.

Some of the suggestions indicated above for Patiala, and later for Bhatinda, may here be found applicable. It is indeed reasonably to be hoped that the improvement of Patiala, and the increasing development of Bhatinda, may lead to progress in this town, and also in larger ones throughout Patiala State,

CHAPTER XXVI.

BHATINDA.

The rapid growth of Bhatinda, in its early years, is naturally explained by its exceptional importance as a Railway junction.

Delay for Town-Planning Scheme.

Some explanation of the arrest of the town's growth in recent years is afforded by the delay—from War and other reasons, only too common throughout the World—in the preparation of the long contemplated Town-planning scheme. It is hoped, however, that this Report, with plan herewith submitted, will be found to meet the essential requirements of all concerned; and that building will therefore be able to proceed, and with energy accumulated from past years.

Need of Road System.

It needs, however, only a brief acquaintance with Bhatinda to see that the comparative arrest of growth has also a deeper cause. For the present town is that of the Railway Junction system too exclusively: and it must not be forgotten that here in India, just as in America and other countries, the development of Railways has not been accompanied by any correspondingly adequate development of the surrounding road-system, but the reverse. The existence from antiquity of the Fort of Bhatinda shows that it was built to control Road-systems broadly corresponding to the present Railway developments; but these old roads have now fallen into decay; indeed so completely that even the road from Bhatinda past the Bhupindra Grain Mill to the Canal Bridge is all but impassable to modern vehicles, and very difficult and slow—thus wasteful—for bullock-carts.

The planning and gradual development of a Road system connecting Bhatinda (1) with the surrounding villages of its immediate district would thus be of great economy and value, to town and villages alike; for without these roads, the advantages of improved irrigation are too largely wasted, in excessive expense and delay of bringing crops to market etc.

(2) Furthermore these local roads require planning in connection with the Trunk roads of the surrounding district—as notably with Badaur, and Kot Kapura. The existing kucha road from Bhatinda to Tappa Station, not far from Bhatinda, is nearly completed (with kanker on sides ready for spreading) and it affords an example of how even such lateral routes may indirectly serve to bring produce and business to Bhatinda.

(3) The opening of existing Canal Roads to local traffic would substantially aid the prosperity of the town; and a reasonable contribution towards their up-keep, by the Roads Department of Patiala State, would thus be found economical, where saving cost of separate road construction.

This question of developing road systems to existing Railway Systems has lately been the subject of a carefully studied Report by

Prof. Stanley Jevons to the U. P. Government, and will here also be found suggestive.

In short, though railways be like arteries, roads are like smaller and larger veins; and both are needed for healthy circulation.

The development of motor communications in and around Bhatinda, is of course at present completely arrested: but as Road Development proceeds, this will develop, and before many years for goods as well as passenger traffic.

Needs of Irrigation: Bhatinda and District.

Excellent though is the general Irrigation system of this province of the State, that of the immediately surrounding Bhatinda Town District is very limited, owing to the abandonment (for reasons I have not been able to discover) of the "Bhatinda Minor", to a mere local water-course. It is now encouraging, however, to be able to report (from particulars explained on official plan by Sardar Charan Singh S. D. O. Canal) that this present water-course (taken from R. D. 186 on right bank of Bhatinda Distributory) is capable of remodelling and exclusion to Bhatinda Town (and with service also to villages on the way) at very moderate expense. A new contour survey is now required, costing say Rs. 4,000, after which the necessary labour will cost from Rs. 4,000 to Rs. 6,000—say, therefore, Rs. 10,000 in all for this section; and capable of execution within three or four months after authorisation by State.

As this water-supply is the one and indispensable condition of the proposed extension and development of Bhatinda, and with its Garden Suburbs, it is earnestly hoped that authorisation for this expenditure, so very moderate in proportion to its results, may now be given. It will also be seen that the taking up of land for homes and gardens in the new suburbs of Bhatinda will soon repay this small capital outlay.

Furthermore, however, it has been explained to me on Irrigation maps that a further continuation of this revised Bhatinda Minor, across the Railway and beyond, will irrigate that still larger rural area, at present dry and with hardly any population, which lies between the Railways and the present Overflow Reservoir in Forest. The Railway crossing arrangements are here comparatively expensive, so that this section is estimated to cost Rs. 14,000 or thereby—making Rs. 24,000 or say quarter of a lakh, for the whole scheme. But as this total outlay irrigates an area of about 8 miles by 4 = 32 square miles, (say well on for 20,000 acres, with deduction for occasional higher areas) it is evidently of the nature of a very profitable investment for the State, as well as of immense advantage to the life and growth of Bhatinda ; and it is thus submitted, and strongly recommended for speedy and favourable consideration. Even if the acres irrigable from this expenditure were only 10,000 (an area surely far below that which will be ascertained after survey) it is evident that the average return from water payments, (averaging Rs. 6 per acre half-yearly for cultivation, and Rs. 7-8 per annum for gardens) makes thus a profitable investment, indeed with surprisingly speedy return of the whole capital outlay of this two-fold scheme—of which both sections—on Bhatinda and opposite sides of Railway—may therefore be carried out at once.

Water needs of Bhatinda Town.

The present water famine, as it practically must almost be called, is now to be mitigated by the approaching completion of the new Diggi as a large tank. But this is incomplete in various ways, and liable also to become a centre of infection; since the poorer classes generally, (and any or all in thirst) will certainly drink this water, as well as use it for washing, etc.

The following precautionary means are, therefore, in my judgment, absolutely necessary—(1) that the water be not brought as at present in open ditch, but in pipe, up to (2) the small range of brick-built channel, which can be inexpensively covered in. (3) The small settling tank, close to the Diggi should be covered, and filled with suitable filtration material; and this renewed, with reasonable frequency, to the satisfaction of the Medical Officer. (4) The people should on no account be allowed to drop their own pots and ropes into the diggi water. This water should be lifted by them in fixed light metal vessels, up to the wall of the diggi, and thence poured into the pots of the individuals, rested on a small low brick platform (about half the height of the wall outside). The metal supports for the needful drawing of water are already erected, but these require a transverse bar, upon either side of which the metal vessels can be fixed.*

Failing this precaution from the outset, supplied before old habits become confirmed, the dipping into the Diggi of a single pot from a household with a cholera case, even before its notification to the Medical Officer, may readily contaminate the water, and spread the disease. Infections of many kinds, (not to speak of ordinary pollutions) will also enter by the ditch, so long as this remains open.

With these precautions, the Diggi will be useful, within a moderate radius. But the length of the town is already so great that the labour and expense of carriage is too severe a burden upon the population, and tends to maintain that poverty of water from which the town has so long suffered.

The adjacent Hindu Tank, now properly constructed and planted with future shade-trees around, is readily capable of connection with the Diggi, this further insuring its cleanliness. On Town-plan herewith will be seen the proposed the union of Tank, Diggi, etc. with a Public Garden. The attractiveness of this area will aid in maintaining the public respect for the purity of their waters; and an efficient mali in charge will practically serve at once as an inspecting and an educational officer.

* An inexpensive model for this purpose is afforded by the private well of that talented Patiala inventor, Sardar Raja Babu, which may possibly be adapted to this place.

Other tanks in Bhatinda.

Just as Hindu piety and public spirit have already built the Tank next *Diggi*, so it will again doubtless lead with regard to the two remaining Tanks.

Disregarding mere temporary and unwholesome pools, which should at once be filled up—(like the large and disgusting mosquito-puddle lying immediately west of Hindu tank) we come next to the small Tank near NW angle of the Fort. Even in its present wretched condition, it is obviously used; and thus deserves renewal and reconstruction, with slight enlargement, as shown on plan.

Finally we come to the larger Tank, that of Old Bhatinda, lying a full quarter mile south of the Fort, and forming the natural centre of this quarter, as shown on new Plan also.

This is at present utterly polluted by the inflow of the Railway drain. But this drain, it may reasonably be hoped, the Railway authorities will be found ready and willing to continue for the necessary moderate distance farther past the tank, and to a point where its outflow can be used for a vegetable garden. The Sanitary authority of Bhatinda will be within its rights, and only performing its duty, in pressing for the removal of this nuisance, which has only arisen during the period, now happily ending, of indifference (on both sides) to public health.

The suggested improvements are broadly indicated on Plan herewith (although as this has been prepared on the old Survey plan of 1902, some fresh survey is of course necessary before execution.)

A clean water connection is necessary for this large tank, to maintain it during the dry season: hence may not a pipe be continued to this also?

Needed Development of Water Supply: Standposts etc.

Here we come to a development essential to the future of the town, and for which I cannot plead too strongly; *viz.* the establishment of a proper and regular water supply by pipe system throughout the whole range of the present and future city, with standposts at moderate intervals, and also admitting of house connections as desired, these latter of course at householders' expense.

My enquiries, both on former and recent visit to Bhatinda, have fully convinced me that the community is not only able, but willing, and even most anxious, to pay such water-rate as the necessary capital and maintenance outlays may require.

These outlays are happily not great for so considerable a population; and are also urgently needed to promote its growth. The necessary outlays for a Filtration plant, pipe system, and standposts at moderate distances, for a future population of (say at least) 40,000 are readily estimated, as also the requisite annual maintenance budget; and it will thus be seen that the resulting water-rate is well within the means of the community. I have never been more repeatedly and emphatically assured of this willingness—even anxiety, to pay water rate: and with obvious explanation—that this rate will be far less than they at present spend, or will have to spend on carriage of water from the Diggi: (and of course in both cases for a supply far inferior, in quantity and in quality alike).

I, therefore, submit this Filtered Water Scheme as essential to city development; and quite apart from that ordinary supply of irrigation water for future Garden-suburbs which the Canal Department can so readily assure to these.

Old Bhatinda Town.

This town is largely kucha, and badly dilapidated at too many points, if not throughout. The narrow streets and lanes are in wretched condition; and some demolitions are inevitable. Notably, first in connection with the opening out of the present Fort entrance, and its new thoroughfares, and latter with the clearing back along the whole south side of Fort, so as to permit carrying an Avenue Road along this distance of over 200 yards, and in keeping with that preservation of open space around the Fort on its other three sides—east, west and north, which it is desired to maintain, indeed gradually to restore, from its many kucha encroachments especially. Hence the needed new Lay-out broadly indicated on plan for extension of old Bhatinda (although as the sand hills, etc. have changed since the 1902 plan, and new permanent buildings also arisen, this sketch will need adjustment, which I shall be ready to make whenever up-to-date survey is forthcoming).

The improvement of the old streets can be done less expensively by use of the broken brick rubbish so abundant throughout the town; while the necessary widening for narrow streets can be afforded by demolishing and clearing away ruins, so as to afford wide "sidings," and sometimes small squares at street crossings, which will be quite sufficient for the moderate local traffic. Further possible developments are indicated on Plan herewith.

The treatment of these ruins on the method fully outlined for Patiala (Chapter XXII) was here quite independently suggested to me (indeed pressed). It would be applicable in old Bhatinda as in Patiala; and as found in town-planning elsewhere.

The tolerance, and even encouragement, of kucha building in the extension of old Bhatinda, is to be recommended, as regards the poorer members of the community, these dispossessed from existing kucha buildings especially. For if this cheap construction be properly regulated, and with adequate courtyard space, it admits of larger rooms than with the more expensive kucha-pukka, and thus of healthy air-space, often otherwise unattainable. The small productivity, frequent ill-health, and consequent poverty of lower-class Indian labour is deeply connected with the insufficient air-space and deficient through ventilation of its dwellings, and often those of kucha-pukka most of all.

Before leaving Old Bhatinda, I must mention that its improvements, much as above indicated, were ably urged upon me by representatives of its older residents; who also desired me to recall in this Report that the expenditure of one lakh for Old Bhatinda Improvement—apart from that of the rest of the town—had received favourable consideration before the War.

Modern Bhatinda : Present Condition.

The original Lay-out has the merits and conveniences of regularity. But its plots and blocks have now for the most part been not only built, but over-built, with over-crowding very prevalent accordingly, and much deficient courtyard air-space. Hence a most unfavourable re-action upon the health of the community; and that of its women and children especially.

There are already a large number of householders alive to this state of things, and anxious for suburban dwellings with gardens accordingly. Such a movement towards suburban life will increase accommodation for shops, and still more that for offices within the present business area (as these latter can be readily accommodated upstairs); so that the present Sadar Bazar area will not need such largely prolonged extension as at first sight seems desirable. The three Bazars at right angles to Sadar Bazar (Masjidwala, Pipalwala and Railway) have also long been developing—and at some points also too closely: still some sites remain for improvement, and especially in Railway Bazar. This will improve as new access to Railway.

Needed Extensions; and Condition of this.

Still some extension of the present Business quarter must be provided for: and still more in view of that influx of traders, and of agencies of business from other towns, which is here so confidently anticipated, as soon as the expansion of the town can proceed.

The essential town-planning condition for any and all successful extensions of business centres is that they be made in direct continuity with the existing Business quarter, and not started apart from this. Hence I have no option but to plan for the lengthening of the main Sadar Bazar line, at both ends.

(A). Extension Southwards.

I am informed that it is proposed—as part of the future improvement of the Railway station—to move the present Goods Shed further southwards: as also to provide a suitably dignified approach to private platform for H.H. the Maharaja. This double improvement is favourable to planning and improvement of the present untidy south end of the Sadar Bazar, and beyond the bend of that main thoroughfare. Hence Plan accordingly; which is left capable of further extension in the future, with increase of grain trade especially.

(B). Extension Northwards.

As the general Town-plan shows, this is the main direction of future Bhatinda development; and not merely, though mainly, for dwellings and garden suburbs, but also for main thoroughfares, towards the Canal, its Bridge etc. and of course also for future industrial and manufacturing development.

Here, therefore, arises especially the problem of "Zoning": *i.e.*, the now established method of broadly allocating specific town areas towards their best respective uses.

Just as the Grain trade has established itself south of present Station entrance, so the great Bhupindra Flour Mill has taken up the proper position beside the Railway northward; and future industrial and manufacturing enterprises will naturally also be provided for along this line, with Railway sidings available; and with housing of their labour as near this as possible to eastward, more or less, as already began by the new dwellings erected in connection with the Flour Mill. Behind this again (*i.e.*, farther eastward) the present large gardens already indicate the beginning of the future Garden-suburbs, which can extend as far as need be, since upon an area mainly commanded by the future Irrigation supply.

Yet central to this whole development is the further northward extension of the Sadar Bazar, and that continuously, as above said.

This extension is at present blocked by the small old building of the Dispensary (1888) with its small and inadequate Hospital accommodation in compound behind. I am thus compelled to recommend the removal of Dispensary and Hospital alike to a more suitable site; with demolition of the present small Dispensary building, and prolongation of the Bazar Street accordingly, as shown on Plan.

Before other features of this planning, it is best here to submit the scheme which reflection and enquiry convince me as of possible substantial service to the re-opening development of Bhatinda—that of instituting a periodic "Bhatinda Fair".

Proposed Bhatinda Fair.

Fairs, Melas, etc.. are long familiar features of Indian life; and these often from great antiquity, and thus largely with religious origin and sanction: yet necessarily, more or less also, with a substantial business-side, since leaving a good deal of money in the centres where they are held.

Many of the great towns of Europe owe their origin to their old Fairs, and sometimes even their continued prosperity to this day, as so notably the great city of Leipzig. And that this old movement is reviving, and upon the modern commercial scale, has of late been strikingly been illustrated at Lyons, where the ancient Fair was revived by its enterprising Mayor during the War from 1916 onwards; and with such success as since to justify and reward the erection of an immense range of Fair and Exhibition buildings. Furthermore, despite the present acute embarassment of German finance, large parliamentary grants, as well as Municipal and private outlays are being made annually to initiate such fairs at important railway centres throughout Germany : and beginnings in this direction are under discussion on British cities, and sometimes even active initiatives also. The type of Fair of course depends upon the regional conditions, and on the commercial and industrial character of the towns and cities within convenient Railway reach. Here in Bhatinda, with its peculiarity wide connections, the general prospects, and the wide variety of such a Fair, are favourable ; indeed beyond most places in India.

The Exhibition of Patiala State products at Madras a few years ago, so successfully conducted there by Pandit Sardar Madho Ram, may here be recalled, as also the corresponding exhibit at present invited by the British Empire Exhibition at London 1924. Yet all such exhibitions have too much of the nature of State display and corresponding sacrifice ; since the geographical situation of the Punjab, with consequent cost of transport, is wellnigh the most unfavourable in India for distant commerce. It is thus for the Bhatinda Fair to concentrate mainly in and for the State, yet to attract visitors and custom from the range of its convenient Railway communication : and these are quite wide enough for its prosperous growth through years to come.

Agricultural products will have the first place—grain of all sorts, cottons, fibres, silk, etc., with manures, implements, etc. In fact a many-sided Agricultural and Cattle Show, with Horticultural Show also. The last named may indeed here be peculiarly stimulating, since where better can one see in India a more striking contrast between what are practically desertic conditions and the fertility of the first rate fruit and vegetable garden next the canal, conducted by Lala Moti Ram.

The second feature of such a Fair is that more popular among townsfolk—the varied range of the stalls of textiles, embroideries, hardware, metal work and cutlery, jewellery, furniture, toys, etc., etc.

Athletic sports are also a standard feature of such gatherings, and readily bring athletes and spectators from far and near. Cricket, football, tennis, hockey, polo, wrestling, running, etc., have each and all their large public.

Cinema and Theatre, Music and Song have also their wide appeals : and in this connection it may be confidently be predicted that the revival of the old plays, music, etc., which were within living memory so much appreciated, may be easy here in India, as we have of late years been finding possible in Europe.

Gatherings for discussion—in fact Congresses—readily arise in connection with all these subjects, with invaluable spread of knowledge and improvements in practice accordingly—as for Agriculture and Stock-breeding, for Agricultural and other Co-operation, for Economic questions, for Education and Sciences, forMusic and Arts, and for Religions and Castes; and of course all with attraction to the Press, and widening appeal of the Fair accordingly.

The excellent institutions known as Vacation Schools or Gatherings, with their varied educational supplies of all kinds—agricultural, musical, etc., also readily arise in connection with such fairs ; and can be housed, like Congresses, etc. in educational or legal buildings, if free for vacation. Failing these, tents are easily provided.

Location of Fair.

The best site in Bhatinda for the pitching of the main tents etc. of this proposed fair is of course the large vacant area opposite the present Station entrance, and free all the way to the Dispensary (*i. e.* Sadar Bazar). I am informed this area is in private hands: but if so, though a moderate margin for improved building is indicated, for the rest its owner can be compensated in an equivalent value of land elsewhere. Such arrangements are of course of the essence of town-planning everywhere.

This area tidied up, and planted as shown on plan, will probably suffice for the Fair in its first years. But later, if all goes well, this area will be insufficient, and may best be reserved for the varied goods of the fair, leaving the area further north, between Thakur Dass' Compound and Dak bungalow and the Flour Mill, for the agricultural fair.

Possible Rise of Auction Mart.

From this periodic agricultural Fair there may before very long reasonably arise a periodic Auction Mart for live stock of all kinds at Bhatinda, at first with quarterly sales, and soon monthly one. Indeed at such junction towns in Europe, as notably in Scotland, weekly sales commonly arise. Again with substantial profit to the town concerned.

Further Extension of Fair.

As the fair grows it may with advantage spread yet further. Thus the best surroundings for a small Horticultural Show may be in the proposed Public Garden shown on plan round the Diggi, Hindu Tank etc., or beyond this, on vacant ground.

The Sports will naturally centre at the large Playing Field shown on plan for new High School, while the Dramatic and Musical functions may be accommodated in the Fort, of which the slopes admit of easy and inexpensive seating for spectators. As to the times for such Fairs, my enquiries lead to suggesting the first fortnights of March and November; but these dates can be adjusted with full local knowledge, and varied as experience may justify.

Tents, I trust, can be partly available on the spot, partly borrowed from Patiala. The main initial outlays will thus be for prizes, for competitions in the various sections of the Fair, for which Rs. 4,000/- or 5,000/- may readily be absorbed: but with good indirect return.

Other Indirect Results of Fair.

Of these I reckon the most substantial to be the attraction to Bhatinda of new business men of all kinds, and from neighbouring provinces as well as Patiala State, in fact that growth of the town by the increase of its men of enterprise, which has been fundamental to the growth of all great commercial and industrial towns, up to Bombay and Karachi, to London and New York. The impulse and enterprise of such incomers soon associates itself with that of the existing community, and with increase of prosperity, and further development of the town accordingly.

Proposed Public Hall, Theatre & Cinema.

Bhatinda lacks amusements for the long evenings; and those who wait at Station between trains have little attraction after walking through the Bazar. A Cinema Hall is therefore indicated, within sight and easy reach of Station Entrance, upon the large and suitable vacant site adjacent to Dak bungalow. Another convenient site may be in main Bazar, near this, as shown on plan. This Hall can readily be adjusted as Theatre also, and for Musical Entertainments, Public Lectures etc.

Proposed Municipal Committee, & Office.

Experience of city life and development, in India as well as Europe, shows that a community of any magnitude such as this, requires a Municipal Committee or Council to attend to its ordinary requirements, as of Water, Sanitation and Cleaning, Lighting etc. etc.; also a Sub-Committee actively interested in its Town-planning and extension. It is encouraging to learn that such development is contemplated by the Patiala Government.

I have been most favourably impressed by the activity and public spirit of Pandit Sardar Madho Ram, Naib Nazim, of Sardar Dhillon, Sardar Qazi Mohammad Suleiman, Dr. Kirpa Ram the resident medical officer, Tehsildar Mohammad Nabi Khan, and other leading men. But their work, and that of so large a town, is now so great as to require the further assistance of public-spirited citizens, and such can readily be found. It is no derogation from the legitimate powers and duties of the central authorities at Patiala, to say that the conducting of local affairs by correspondence with the capital is too slow and un-economic. The constitution of a Municipal Committee will thus be a welcome relief to the tasks of the Ijlas-I-Khas, though this will of course conserve all essential powers of control, inspection, appeal, etc.

Suggested Municipal Office.

I, therefore, suggest the neighbourhood of Dak Bungalow as the most suitable location for Municipal (and Town Planning) Office; for though at present at the extremity of the town, it stands, as the plan shows, near its future centre. Police accommodation may be found at the Magistrates' Court Building, by division or by addition.

Boys' High School, and Girls' High School.

This High School building, though fairly recent, belongs too much to the old style of too purely literary education, and is lacking in those facilities for laboratory, workshop and garden instruction, which are each and all so essential to the newer movement of education on which the world is now everywhere entering. And though as yet in India too slowly, yet here also; and especially in a town like Bhatinda, where practical and technically competent men are required, and not more condidates for the overcrowded literary and legal sides of the University.

Moreover the Playing-ground is quite inadequate: and I therefore suggest that the best use which can be made of this present High School will be to hand it over as a Girls' High School, for which its class-rooms and playing-space are more sufficient; and before this, to erect, as soon as funds allow, a larger Boys' High School, with more ample Playing Fields, a little further away, as indicated on Plan.

Electric Lighting.

For this there is no fear of ample demand. One (no doubt sanguine) estimate I received was of "5000 shops and houses anxious for light:"and another as to electric fans— "say 200." On enquiry as to the future of small industries using electric power, "probably 50 or more" might soon have to be provided for. Without of course pressing such high figures, there can be no doubt that Bhatinda is ready and anxious for electric lights, fans and local power. Here too the conditions are promising. The Turbine and Dynamo plant of Mr. Lala Moti Ram beside the Canal are a good earnest of this; and when as hoped the present fall of the Canal is improved, to 12 (or even 16) ft., I am informed that some 400 h. p. would become available for the electrical supply of the city.

Possible Tramway.

The Monorail Tramway at Patiala did not pay; but this might have been predicted from its irregular Town plan, with no single central route. Here, however, in Bhatinda, this central thoroughfare exists, and is the axis of future extension. If this Monorail plant be capable of adaptation here, is it not probable that it would soon be paying? European and other experience shows that low fares pay best; and there must already be many in Bhatinda, and this especially as the Sadar Bazar is lengthened, who would gladly save time and strength by paying ½ anna fare for the length of the town (and some even an anna for first class section of car). The main traffic would of course be in the town itself, but as this extends at both ends, especially towards the Canal, so would the line: with (say) hourly, and by and by more frequent, trips so far; and of course at increased fare, say 1 anna second class and 1½ to 2 annas first class.

Bhatinda Industries.

These are at present too limited in number. But even the present staples admit of increase of these. Thus at this agricultural and railway centre, with increasing movement of stock, the Slaughter house at the Southern limit of the town might be extended; and have refrigerating cars on the way to Lahore etc.

The trade in Hides may also be developed; and though the climate, and water-scarcity still more, have discouraged tanning, something of this may yet arise.

A Bonecrushing Mill in Bhatinda would also yield phosphate manure for farms and gardens.

Wool is already of importance; and one good cloth-weaving establishment exists. Why not by and by more?

Why not carpets etc ?

Silk with all its developments, may come in, when irrigation makes mulberry-leaves abundant.

Vegetable and Fruit-growing are already profitable, as Mr. Moti Ram's garden shows: and the irrigable district, as mentioned at the outset, is so large as to admit of supplying needs far beyond those of Bhatinda Town, though that large local demand is not to be despised.

The clay for Pottery is said to be very good. So why not here import one or two of the skilled potters from Sind with their beautiful blue-glaze ware, from here so much more easily distributed than from Sind itself ?

Similarly for Carpet-weaving. Similarly too for Kashmir Furniture and Carving, for its beautiful Papier-mache colour-work, its famous Embroideries, and so on. In short why not establish such industries in Bhatinda as would give its minor produce an artistic character, and reputation accordingly.

Finance of Town-planning Scheme.

The immediate source of revenue is of course by the sale of plots of land for extension purposes. The rates fixed should be moderate, so as to encourage development, and to dispose of a large area on moderate terms as speedily as may be. The holding up of land is statistically proven to be far from profitable on the whole, despite occasional instances to the contrary.

I am moreover informed that a large sum—of some 10 lakhs or thereby—was raised by the Bhatinda Committee before the war. If this be so, here are substantial funds available.

The large sums deposited by the Court of Wards, and other funds in State Treasury, also afford capital towards building advances; and on the best possible class of security.

Co-operative Building Societies on the various models indicated by Indian and European town-extension experience, as at Bombay, London etc. etc. may be considered with advantage.

Improvement of Timber and Fuel Supply.

This extension of Bhatinda Town will naturally interest the State Forestry Department, which may here not only dispose of timber to advantage, but may be encouraged to such further Timber-planting, and also to such fuel-planting as its convenient areas may allow. May not individual investors also be encouraged to take up land for planting ?

As a beginning, may not the present melancholy contrast of the dry and treeless aspect of Bhatinda with the verdant and shady Railway Settlement opposite, be used by the Forest Department as an argument for the increased extension of its activities in this neighbourhood ?

The Canal Department can readily indicate to the Forest Department all areas not commanded by its proposed irrigation scheme, yet henceforth less dry also, and thus more suitable for fuel-planting (kikar etc,) than heretofore. Thus too the present dust-storms may be substantially abated.

Agricultural Trees: Date, Fig etc.

Principal Milne, of the Agricultural College, Lyallpur, has been able to introduce, and with fair prospect of success, these inestimable date-palms which are the base of Bassorah trade, and also the figs which are so pre-eminent of Smyrna. I plead for as full trial of these, and other fine varieties of fruit-bearing trees, as can be arranged for.

Essential Condition of City Development.

All these schemes for Bhatinda, as for Patiala, or other cities anywhere, will be found to depend not only on natural conditions, or on general progress, or on the necessary finance, or on State approval and patronage—though all these are necessary, and are repeatedly emphasised above. They also depend upon the men responsible at each point, in general capacity and character, and in particular interest and skill for each development of this many sided work; and on the measure of interest, sympathy, and practical co-operation accordingly which they can arouse in others. Bhatinda, like Patiala, is fortunate in having such men—of whom some are already named above: and, with encouragement from the State, I have no doubt they will soon find active co-operation towards the development of this community from among its leading members.

P. G.